Sell Like a Boss: A Complete Guide to Blow Up Your Sales ... *How Top Sales People Sell Differently and You Can Too*

ARCHIE T. GOLDBACKER

Copyright © 2017 Archibald Tutmoses Goldbacker

All rights reserved.

ISBN: 1542464293
ISBN-13: 978-1542464291

DEDICATION

This book is dedicated to all aspiring sales professionals who are striving hard day after day to achieve extraordinary goals.

Table of Contents

	Page
Who Should Read this Book	1
Why Should I Learn from You	1
But Sales is a Low Brow Profession	2
Is Marketing the Same as Sales	4
Evolution of Marketing	4
Selling Ice to Innuit	6
What's Worth Selling & How Good is the Soil	6
The Tripod of Sales Success	9
THE SELF	10
I'm not Cut Out for Sales	10
Goal Orientation	11
Grit	11
The Elevator to Success	12
You are not Inferior in the Buyer-Seller Dynamic	13
Distraction is Destruction	14
Confidence	14
Positivity v Realism v Negativity	15
Guarding your Time & E-mail Sanfus	15
Do Only that Which Only You Can Do	17
Always be Learning	18
Be Humble with Pride	20
Workout	21
Leverage Technology	22
Communication is the Lubricant	23
Stop Using the Same Stale Adjectives	25
Prioritize or Die	26
Sense of Urgency & the Illusion of Sales Solipsism	27
THE CLIENT	29

The Client in B2C	30
The Client in B2B	35
Qualifying Prospects	36
Initial Call or the Dreaded Cold Call	38
Voicemails, E-Mails, or Texts? Tricks of the Trade	41
The Dump Message	44
Personal Cell Phone Numbers are Gold	45
Birthdays and Thank You	45
Should I Buy Lists?	46
Warm Calls	47
Know the Trident	48
Preparing for the Meeting	50
The Meeting	51
Account Penetration	57
The Magic Portfolio	58
Listening Skills: The Power of the F-Bomb	58
Empathy	59
The Client is not your Friend	60
Connect the Dots & Show them the Way	61
To Lunch or not to Lunch	63
Compress the Sales Cycle or I'm okay with a "No"	63
A Word on Trade Shows	64
A Word on Commitment	64
A Word on Humor	66
The Opportunity (or Potential)	66
Time, Timeline, and Money	71
Who is the Shot Caller - the Mistake Every Salesperson Makes	75
Bypassing Pseudo-Decision Makers	77

Proposal Hell or Why I don't write Proposals	78
Closing or Make Sure to Ask for the Sale	80
Price is Rarely the Main Issue & How Not to Drop Your Pants	81
The Universe of Objections and How to Overcome Them	84
The Problem of Anchoring	86
How to Get Paid Quickly or Show Me the Scrilla	87
Disinvite Legal from the Party	89
Recency, Frequency, and Dollar Amounts	90
Clients Like Talking about Themselves	91
If you Sense it Say it (Tactfully)	92
Communication is the Lubricant Redux	94
THE COLLEAGUE	96
Good Bosses and Bosses from Hell	96
Operations	104
Other Salespeople	105
Partner Relationships	105
Suppliers	105
Assistants	106
Elite Sales People versus Mediocre Sales People	107
A Word on Business Development & Strategy for Sales	110

Treat People with Respect and Dignity	110
Mavens, Connectors, and Great Salespeople	111
The One Year Look Back or Analyze This	112
Vision and Mission	113
What is my Promise?	114
Distribution Channels and an Ecosystem of Relationships	114
Pivoting on your Products & Services	114
Lead and Disrupt	115
Final Thoughts	116

ACKNOWLEDGMENTS

There are far too many people who have contributed to the knowledge I have attempted to impart in this book. I owe a debt of gratitude to luminaries such as erudite sales master Randy Webb, sales scholar Michael Ahearne, preeminent salesman Dwight Lamar Keys, technopreneur Dipesh Desai, and last but not least a man of all ages and connector par excellence Dr. Phil Rogers.

Who Should Read this Book?

- People who are new to sales and are curious to learn the key principles
- Entrepreneurs who aren't sure how to generate revenue
- Anyone who needs to sell a product, idea, or service
- People who are curious about the profession and what it entails
- Salespeople who want to become top producers
- Top producers who want to sharpen their repertoire
- Executives who interact with sales people

Why Should I Learn from You?

I have been in the sales profession for almost two decades and have seen it all. In a multi-national company with a global sales force of hundreds of sales people I achieved President's Club multiple times as well as attained a top five global ranking selling millions of dollars of services. My clients ranged from small-to-medium sized businesses all the way to sophisticated buyers in Fortune 500 companies. I started from the very beginning in sales and learnt all the tricks you can employ and all the mistakes you should avoid in order to be among the best. Believe it or not I've seen rookie mistakes that even senior sales people make.

As I advanced in my career I consulted for various companies and noticed the same set of mistakes that rookies made and the same set of best practices to which the top performers adhered. In this book I have distilled for you the most important principles that will make a huge difference in your ability to sell. I will also teach you methods that only the very elite sales people employ. If you follow these principles I promise you that you'll be able to close more deals, shorten the sales cycle, be less frustrated in your career, and actually derive pleasure in this profession – not to mention generate increased income. If you can close even two more deals a month because of principles you apply from this book imagine how much added income that is to you annually.

But Sales is a Low Brow Profession, Why Should I Learn it?

That's a seemingly good question. The reality is that some of the highest earners in the economy are sales people. With an average annual income (as of 2014) of $65,800 and with the top 10% easily earning above $100,000 the career prospects are excellent. Demand for good sales people is always strong. Professional sales is not one of those careers that will be automated away into oblivion because there is a nuanced human touch required. There has been a recent proliferation of marketing automation companies, which are geared towards inbound marketing, lead generation, and e-Commerce where a sale does not require a high-touch approach. However, there are just too many products and services where a sales person plays a crucial role in guiding the buyer through closure.

Go to any job board and you'll always find sales positions open in Fortune 500 companies. Most of the successful sales people I know earn six figures and some earn seven figures. Some sales people go on to become CEOs in Fortune 500 companies or start their own bustling businesses.

Mark Cuban, the flamboyant billionaire, in late 2016 stated that if he lost all his wealth and had to start over he would get a sales job during the day because he could get duly compensated. Cuban started off early in his life selling baseball cards and stamps and progressed to selling computers and software. Cuban has a wonderful saying that applies to business: "When your back's against the wall, sales cures all." He declared about his sales skills: "I was the best. I crushed it." You can view more in his video entitled "If I had to start over here's what I would do."

CEOs wear many hats and being the company's chief sales person is one. When Boeing sells a multi-billion dollar order to a government it's the CEO who is the chief sales person in that deal. Consider technology magnate Larry Ellison of Oracle. Even after he became a billionaire he kept his finger on the pulse by overseeing potential deals. Steve Jobs, a singular genius, was also an excellent pitchman. While he wasn't going door to door selling he wowed his audience on stage at product launches and whetted the appetites of masses like no other Apple representative could. There is a long list of famous sales people who went on to become very wealthy through their passion and keen understanding of sales. Just google "famous sales people" to get an idea of phenomenally successful people you didn't even think were sales people.

Having said that, monetary rewards may not be what drives you to a sales career. There are people who are intrinsically motivated and genuinely enjoy adding customer value or making a difference. Find what motivates you and anchor your work from that base.

Is Marketing the Same as Sales?

Think of marketing as the platform that is necessary for sales to occur. Marketers analyze the market, the customers (who will buy?), the distribution channels (through what channels do I get the product into the customer's hands?), and they segment the market into different groups and inform the sales people where to focus for profitable selling. In that sense, marketers and sales people are like a sniping team with marketers acting as the spotter and the sales person playing the role of triggerman. Each has their very important but uniquely different roles. If you're a great marketer that does not mean you will be a great sales person and vice versa.

Marketing is what brings you into the car dealership in the first place by creating awareness. Sales is what makes you leave the dealership with the car.

Evolution of Marketing

Marketers have segmented the various eras into the following timelines and categories. I will focus on the current era in this book but it's good to know the different eras. For a more detailed treatment visit Dr. White's site dstevenwhite dot com and search the terms "The Evolution of Marketing."

Simple Trade Era (from the beginning of mankind until 1850's) – this era was marked by trade of goods and resources (cotton, spices, silk, etc.)

Production Era (1860's to 1920's) – driven by the industrial revolution products were mass produced and demand was ample because there weren't enough competitors.

Sales Era (1920's to 1940's) – an influx of competitors made price the major factor in buying decisions making this an era of commoditization.

Marketing Department Era (1940's to 1960's) – this era emerged due to consumers having higher buying power by virtue of higher discretionary income so businesses systematized disparate marketing activities into a formal marketing department leading to phrases we still see today like "new and improved!"

Marketing Company Era (1960's to 1990's) – this era saw a paradigm shift in which customers were viewed as the reason for the existence of a business and all employees served marketing goals in some way. Phrases like "customer is king" and "the customer is always right" emerged during this era and in some ways this era has continued till today.

Relationship Marketing Era (1990's to 2010) – building trust became paramount. Forming life-long relationships with the customer was the thrust of this era. Use of technology like CRM (customer relationship management) software took off.

Social/Mobile Marketing Era (2010's to Present) – developing upon the tenets of the relationship marketing era this era seeks to be connected to the customer constantly.

There are overlaps between the various eras and concepts from eras that intertwine and permeate the marketing ethos today. The social/mobile marketing era in my opinion is a subset of the relationship marketing era that is specific to the consumer market – by that I mean where businesses sell to consumers (also known as B2C). The social/mobile marketing techniques have not caught on in the business to business (B2B) sales arena as well as in the B2C market. An example of B2C sales is Nike selling shoes to the general consumer. An example of B2B sales is Microsoft selling enterprise software to the IT department at General Electric.

Selling Ice to Inuit

Some people think that a good sales person is one who can sell anything to anyone or sell the proverbial ice to Inuit and wine to teetotalers. Some books even claim to teach you to sell anything to anyone. The problem with that is you cannot sustainably maintain sales and you cannot even begin to foster a long term relationship with a customer if you are not adding value to a customer's life. Customers today aren't ignorant. Rather, they are sophisticated buyers with a wealth of information handy before you even sit at the table. Preparation and understanding the customer is of paramount importance. Understanding the ecosystem around the customer is something the top sales people master. I'll cover that in more detail in the "Tripod of Sales Success" section of the book.

What's Worth Selling and How Good is the Soil?

This is an important question to consider before you join a company as a sales person. If you are interviewing for a sales position know that you are interviewing the company just as they are interviewing you. You are going to invest significant effort and time (and opportunity cost) to grow your client base when you join a company. You are the one who will be planting the seeds but you need to do your due diligence on whether the soil is fertile. Below I list some crucial things to keep in mind.

1) Is the product/service you are going to sell commoditized or late in the product maturity cycle i.e. dying out? A product or service is commoditized when buyers cannot distinguish between your product and that of a competitor because there are few if any differentiators between your product and that of your

competitor. If you sell a bushel of wheat and farmer Joe sells a bushel of wheat, guess what? You will both sell it at the exact same price. The market does not care that your wheat grew basking in the sun in land irrigated by rainwater. If you join a company where the product is almost commoditized your only way to success is volume of sales and your company needs to have the lowest price point among all competitors. You will not be able to employ your sales skills in such an environment and you will be at the market's mercy. You will become an "order taker." How do you know if you're late in the product maturity cycle? If you joined Blackberry as its sales were tanking and iPhones took off then you know Blackberry had ridden its wave and was approaching the end of its cycle. Be acutely aware of the signs of the maturity of a product.

2) Differentiation is important in your ability to be able to capture the customer's attention. Does the accounting software you're selling make it much easier for the customer to generate a purchase order or does it force the customer through an uncomfortable set of steps? If so, the customer needs to know.

3) Is the management in good shape or is there massive turnover? Go to glassdoor dot com and read the reviews to get an idea. Poor management will impair your ability to sell even if the product is great. Usually this comes in the form of long-winded processes, bureaucratic inefficiencies, or meaningless roadblocks.

4) Ask to speak to other sales people in the company to get an understanding of what's working well and what's challenging.

5) If you are unsure about whether the product or service is commoditized or not talk to an experienced mentor.

Finding a mentor is extremely important because you'll advance much more quickly and avoid pitfalls.
6) What's really going on inside a company? If the company you want to join is privately owned you'll just have to ask the interviewer and other employees if they let you talk to them. If the company you want to join is publicly traded you are in luck (a publicly traded company has stock that trades on an exchange). Go to the 'Investors' section of their website and then click on 'SEC Filings' and scroll down until you find something called the 10-K form. Download it and go to the Management Discussion & Analysis (MD&A) section and you'll find out a lot of the challenges the company is facing and whether it is growing or shrinking and you'll even find out which product lines are most profitable (or not profitable at all). 10-K reports are very useful whether you are going in for an interview or a sales call. I have advised sales people to avoid joining a particular company because their 10-K revealed they were in shambles or had not turned a profit in years or were selling antiquated products that were getting crushed by competitors.

In summary, you need to ensure the soil is fertile before you plant the seeds. In the rest of the book I will elaborate upon how you plant the seeds and harvest the fruits of your labor.

The Tripod of Sales Success

Once you've joined a company where the soil is fertile the tripods of your success will come into play. The tripod consists of three "legs" – the self, the client, and the colleagues.

1 THE SELF

Managing the "self" is half the battle in sales. As the Japanese proverb goes - fall seven times get up eight. I have seen hundreds of sales people quit or get fired because they could not manage their "self". When they fell they did not want to get back up. Often they quit just as they were on the verge of success. They quit just when they were about to finish climbing the hill. You cannot control things that are external to you but you can control your reaction to things that happen to you. Cultivate equanimity in your life as much as possible. Below I'll cover some of the challenges that the "self" poses and some of the areas all sales people can strive to improve with regards to the "self."

I'm not Cut out for Sales and I'm an Introvert and I'm not Good Looking

I can't help you with the last one but you don't need dashing good looks or extroversion to be good at sales. I'm a born introvert. I like me-time and prefer a book to large gatherings of people. It's not about introversion or extroversion. The most important factors you need to be successful at sales are goal-orientation and grit. Everything else you can learn and un-learn. People are not born to sell but learn to sell.

Even if you do not want sales as a career just know that every day you are selling something. You are selling your significant other on why it would be better to vacation in Barcelona this year instead of Bali. You are selling your boss an idea that if adopted would result in your team saving hundreds of hours of wasteful work each year. You are selling yourself and your unique abilities in a job interview with a recruiter who is interviewing several other people who use the same buzz words and have the same experience as you. These are examples of "non-sales selling" which is what human beings do 40% of the time without even realizing it. Sales, therefore, is part and parcel of everyone's life.

Goal Orientation

Every good sales person has a goal. The goal might be to sell $20,000 a month or $200,000 a month. It could be to earn $150,000 in commissions this year. It could be to have 20 client meetings a month. It's important to establish a goal by which you can measure your progress and derive satisfaction at achieving it. Excellent sales people are highly goal-oriented. It's your yard-stick that you measure yourself by, not to mention your managers who will also measure your performance by specific metrics like quota.

Grit

Grit is to hang on to the path to achieving your goals no matter what comes your way. It is passionate perseverance. This does not mean you cannot experience sadness, anger, disappointment, or anything negative. You can and you will. But grit requires you to overwhelm your negative emotions with a positive and determined will. If you lose two deals this month, you can be amongst the quitters and say "I'm done, this is too hard" or you can be among the winners and say "you win some, you lose some, so what? Let's move on to the next deal." In sales, overcoming rejection is the essence of grit. The way I was taught once is that you have a price to pay for every deal you win and that is tens of rejections. If you keep that in mind then every rejection is paving the way for the eventual win. Also, re-frame your rejections mentally: the prospective buyer did not reject you because they personally hate you – it just wasn't a good match. Excellent sales people are gritty. You gain tremendous freedom in life when you take nothing personally.

The Elevator to Success

There is neither an elevator nor an escalator to success. You have to climb the stairs just like every successful person. You have to coach your "self" constantly that you get what you put in i.e. your efforts correlate to your success. If you plant 1,000 seeds your harvest is almost assuredly going to be higher than if you plant 10 seeds. It is a numbers game and it requires hard work. Going the extra mile is extremely important when you are new to sales or new to building your client base. In my first year in sales I worked at least 10 hours a day which later tapered down as I built my client base and as I learnt how to work smartly. But going the extra mile is very important early in your career. However, don't despair. I'll share with you all the tricks of the trade to ensure that you don't have to work from 8 am to 8 pm daily. During my years of sales success I was the sales person who used to work the least but I made darn sure that while I was working I was laser focused and followed methodology. I found out later that a lot of the most successful sales people aren't the ones that are working the most. I also observed sales people who did things in 3 hours that I could do in half an hour (I'll share some of these secrets later in this section). The moral is that you have to work hard but in a smart way.

You are not Inferior in the Buyer-Seller Dynamic

You have to think of sales as a value exchange. You have something of value to someone else and you will give that something to that someone in exchange for something of value to you. This takes many forms. For example, you could be a statistician who creates actuarial tables that are of value to your employer which is an insurance company that needs to know how long a customer is expected to live or how frequently they are expected to have an accident. You are selling your labor as a statistician and exchanging that for a salary - this is a value exchange between two parties – you and your employer. You could be a fur trader who exchanges fur for spice. You want the spice for your own consumption or to take it to your homeland to sell and your counter-party wants your fur to take to some winter-land to sell or use. The two parties exchange what is of value to each.

The value exchange is the underlying "truth" or undercurrent of sales and sets up what should be the proper power dynamic. Often times I see sales people groveling or acting apologetic or having a submissive tone when talking to clients. An egregious example was a sales person who offered a client a visit to an exotic gentleman's club in exchange for a sale. Another example that made me shake my head was a salesperson begging the client for a sale because he had to make a mortgage payment on his house. These sales people were not aware of the proper power dynamic between sales person and buyer and here it is – a value exchange is occurring where you, the client, are paying me, the sales person, for something that will add value in your life so we are equal partners in this trade and transaction. There is a saying that "power buys from power" and an equally potent saying that "if you are not ready to walk, you are not ready to talk". Both of these teach sales people that they are not inferior in the buyer-seller dynamic. In fact, if you project power and confidence, you are actually more likely to close the sale because "power buys from power." Furthermore, if you are not ready to walk away from a deal if it's not a win-win for both parties, then you are not "ready to talk" which means you are not ready to negotiate and win a deal with a client if you are desperate for the deal.

Bottom line – the buyer and the seller are on equal footing in a sale. If you think otherwise, you will act otherwise, and you'll lose your dignity and lose deals more frequently.

Distraction is Destruction

If you are busy surfing the net or spending time on social media or exchanging text messages on your phone constantly at work you will not reach the elite level in sales. How do I know? Because I've seen employees like that and they are mediocre at best. If you must access any of these for whatever reason, allocate 5 or 10 minutes during your break time to do so.

Confidence

Confidence typically increases with knowledge or with age or with experience but it is something you must cultivate. There are a number of TED Talks (ted dot com) where experts discuss this topic. I encourage anyone with confidence issues to pay attention to confidence-enhancing techniques because it goes back to the power-dynamic with buyers. Buyers will easily sniff out a person who lacks confidence or hesitates. If you lack confidence you will unwittingly project that to your product or service and your sales will suffer.

Positivity versus Realism versus Negativity

We all feel negative once in a while but what I can't stand is seeing sales people who are always negative about their prospects to sell something or negative about the client or about their colleagues or who make broad-stroke negative pronouncements on a deal in the works. When I hear a sales person say a deal won't close I always ask "how do you know?" and then they will make a pronouncement to which the next logical question again is "how do you know?" and finally you realize the sales person is simply being negative and making huge guesses without valid information to back them up. Don't let negativity ruin your day or your career. A lot of negative sales people think they are realists when in fact they are simply pessimistic. Negative sales people are also rarely successful. Pivot to positivity as much as possible because this connects to grit which I mentioned earlier in the book. There is a lot of material on positive psychology which you can read or watch videos on if you have tendencies toward negativity. Trust me, it will make a difference.

Having said that elite sales people have highly refined radars on what's real and what's not. They have cultivated 'red herring' meters on deals which they have honed with years of experience. Those meters are a healthy mixture of positivity and mild cynicism which ought to not be confused with negativity and pessimism.

Guarding your Time and E-mail Snafus

This is one of the most important points in this book. Elite sales people are fiercely protective of their time because they understand time is money. You have a limited number of hours in a day and a limited number of days in a year. Make the most of every minute of your day. As a sales person if you aren't doing something to progress towards a sale then you are wasting time. This includes administrative hamster-on-wheel "busy work" that is meaningless (like bureaucratic paperwork), or long proposals you have to type up, or filling out expense reports, or chit-chatting with your colleagues at the water cooler about the current hot show on television, or engaging in office intrigue and gossip, or aimlessly surfing the web or social media. Every minute you waste on these non-sales work is money out of your pocket you could have gained from selling. Here are some tips to help guard your time:

- Don't talk excessively to your colleagues.
- Use your e-mail program's Calendar feature to book meetings with clients.
- Book meetings with clients back to back so you aren't driving back and forth from office to client. For example if meeting with Client A is from 10 am – 11 am and client B is 15 minutes from Client A then try to book a meeting with client B at 11:30 am so as to minimize back and forth travel. I always try to stack my meetings back to back for efficiency. You end up saving tons of time over the span of a year.
- Do not spend hours researching a client. I take 30 seconds to 2 minutes (if that) researching any given client unless I am meeting them in which case I will spend a bit more time. Usually I want to know what industry they are in and what services/products they sell. More on that later in the book.
- Do not spend more than 5 minutes writing an e-mail to any given client. 5 minutes really should be the maximum except in extenuating circumstances. Most of the e-mails I write to clients take me 10 to 20 seconds. Clients do not like lengthy e-mails! They already receive

100 e-mails a day and are thankful when they receive a short e-mail. Guess what else? The shorter my e-mail the higher the response rate from clients! If they cannot see what you have written within their computer screen i.e. if you force them to have to scroll down to read the entire e-mail then your e-mail will not get read no matter how cute or decorated. This is something even senior sales persons struggle with because sales people are naturally gregarious and like to talk but e-mails need to be succinct. Use the template features in your e-mail program to generate one-click e-mail responses. This is a huge time saver! Figure out the most common types of e-mails you send to a client and write out templates for each of them and then voila, a large number of the e-mails you end up "writing" will just be one-click templates. Since MS Outlook is a popular e-mail program, google "email templates in Outlook" to see how you can create a template. If you're a Gmail user then google "email templates in Gmail" and you'll get step by step directions. Try to end most of your e-mails with a call-to-action or a call to next steps unless it's a service fulfillment e-mail where you are thanking the client.

Do Only That Which Only You Can Do

This is one of my favorite sayings – do only that which only you can do, delegate the rest. In a sales context it means administrative or "busy work" that is not sales related is anathema. You are costing yourself money and wasting time if you spend more than a modicum of time on non-sales related activities. This includes filling out expense reports, writing reports on something, meeting with your colleagues just for the sake of meeting, fulfilling the services or product order, etc. In many companies sales people spend a considerable amount of time in such administrative tasks but it really ends up costing the company money in lost sales! When I figured this out I hired assistants. My sales doubled the next 12 months. Did my hiring of assistants cause my doubling of sales? Causation is difficult to prove but the strong correlation was good enough for me and good enough for the bosses who picked up the tab for the assistants. How do you get the boss to pick up the tab for assistants? Quantify how much profit your sales brings to the company each year. If you don't have access to profit data then just use sales figures. Then quantify the percentage of time you focus on non-sales related activities that can be handled by an admin assistant. Now it's an easy leap to show your boss how much the company is losing in profits (or sales) because your time is tied up in things you shouldn't even be touching. Then quantify how much having an assistant will cost the company. Your numbers will show exactly the tipping point where it's costing the company and yourself more money to not have an assistant. For e.g. your arithmetic should show that if you spend more than 3.6 hours of time on non-sales related work your company is losing money by not leveraging your expert skills in sales. For every sales person this number will be different but do the math and then have a conversation with the bosses.

Always be Learning

Learning is a lifelong endeavor. As a sales person you must strive to learn from every deal – what worked, what did not, etc. In addition, I highly encourage people to learn by reading books, taking professional development courses, MOOCs, or watching informative videos. You'll pick up something that you can apply in your career. Sales people who don't learn constantly tend to stagnate and plateau. Try to learn about how companies work, how industries work, how money flows in the economy, how you can improve your weaknesses, etc. As you read and learn more you'll find that these come into play in client conversations and they'll appreciate you more as a knowledgeable advisor whom they trust and not simply a transactional "sales rep." Here are some books that I recommend:

- Managing Oneself by Peter F. Drucker
- Good to Great by Jim Collins
- Built to Last by Jim Collins
- Fault Lines: How Hidden Fractures Still Threaten the World Economy by Raghuram Rajan
- The Innovator's Dilemma by Clayton M. Christensen
- Verbal Judo: The Gentle Art of Persuasion by George Thompson
- The 4-Hour Work Week by Timothy Ferriss
- Deep Work: Rules for Focused Success in a Distracted World by Cal Newport
- Little Red Book of Selling by Jeffrey Gitomer
- Any book by Harvard Business Review

These are mostly business books but to be well-rounded learn from other disciplines as well including science, psychology, and economics. The point here is the more well-read you are the more well-rounded you will be and your clients will respect you for it and you'll be able to connect the dots better. Bill Gates is reputed to read one book a week despite being one of the busiest people in the world. Just pick your books wisely. No point in reading books on how to chase down leprechauns in Ireland. If you're too pressed for time you can download an app called Blinkist which summarizes hundreds of books for you in 30-second to 15-minute snippets which you can read or listen. I personally use it and find it very useful to complement my regular book readings.

If you prefer reading magazines or newspapers the best ones to keep your pulse on the business world are the Wall Street Journal, the Financial Times, and The Economist.

I have heard gratifying comments from clients of mine who said "I'm just trying to be like you" and "I have never met a sales rep who knew more about our company than you." This isn't merely for bragging rights but it reduces the resistance of a client to a sale. How can you elicit similar responses? I'll cover more of that in the "The Clients" section of the book.

Be Humble with Pride

This sounds like an oxymoron. What I mean is have pride and dignity in your profession and your own self and your credibility but be humble enough to admit and learn from your mistakes. You will sleep well at night if you know you are really providing something of value to your clients and that you are equal partners with your client. What about being humble? Sales people tend to be type A personalities and some are a little rough around the edges. The top guys tend to be aloof and some are even cocky. Always check your ego and be humble enough to consider other options. The most knowledgeable salesperson in the world still can learn from others who know things he does not because knowledge is a river and you can only drink from it but a little.

I have had frustrating discussions with senior sales reps who are completely unwilling to change or mend their ways because of their clinging to the status quo or because their flawed sales techniques have "worked" in the past and they don't want to try anything new to enhance or sharpen their skills. You cost yourself money when you don't try new things. At least be humble enough to consider that another way might lead to increased sales. If you try it and it fails that's fine. But if you try and you succeed then your humbleness and open mindedness helped you. Once as a senior sales person I was at a sensitive impasse with a client and I talked to another elite sales guy for a fresh set of eyes and ears on the situation. He made an innovative suggestion which I implemented and it resolved the issue successfully and led to a long lasting relationship with the client.

Always be open to suggestions and even if you don't implement all the suggestions you might pick up some valuable nuggets of wisdom.

Workout

This is a non-traditional advice to sales people but I've seen a lot of the top guys do some form of physical activity or hobby whether to blow off steam or get rejuvenated. Rejuvenation is really important for the soul and helps prevent burn out. Pick up some physical activity whether it is walking, jogging, golf, or some sport where you're out and about. Walking, although not strenuous, has been shown to be therapeutic and surprisingly helps with neurogenesis. In lay speak – aerobic exercises and even walking helps you against mental decline and memory loss. Exercise triggers neurogenesis – the birth of new brain cells. Why is this important? Working out will help keep your mind sharp.

I have seen sales people struggle to remember what's going on in deals with customers and sometimes even the customer's name. I'm talking about actual deals in the works with customers they have met in person! I've seen sales people struggle to remember to do crucial follow up activities or struggle to remember names of clients while leaving voicemails or forget important points in client meetings. Don't let that be you. Ward off cognitive decline by engaging in physical activity. Even walking daily can have a significant impact on your mental acuity.

Leverage Technology

Technology is a means that can work for you or against you. Use the technology tool kit that is available to you. This can include e-mail programs (already discussed), productivity apps on your phone, and your CRM (Customer Relationship Management) software. CRM usage is now widespread amongst sales people but I've encountered sales persons in Fortune 100 companies who are resistant to using their CRM. The company's selection of a CRM is very important. Sales people should not feel like they are being hampered when they are using a CRM. There are tens of CRMs in the market now. A CRM is a tool to help you manage and record your interactions with customers and track deals in a systematic way. The grander goal of CRMs is to help sustain business relationships and increase customer loyalty. Most CRMs are intuitive to use and training is available through the vendor or third parties to help you learn how to use it. Behind the scenes, a CRM consists of databases with fields where you can slot in information such as the client name, phone number, e-mail address, activities, potentials (opportunities), meetings, events, pipelines, etc. A CRM helps you manage your deals and activities on a day to day basis and to help you forecast how much you'll be selling in the next 30 to 90 days.

Common CRMs include Salesforce, Microsoft Dynamics CRM, SugarCRM, Zoho, and others. Salesforce is quite popular and has one of the highest adoption rates. A lot of CRMs are free up to a certain number of records. A good free CRM is Zoho which is web-based and lets you use up to 25,000 records free of charge with a 10 user-count limit. If you exceed that you are forced to upgrade or delete records. For a small business with less than 10 sales persons and 1 or 2 sales managers Zoho is a good option.

You can even send slick e-campaigns from within the CRM and track a list of customers that opened and clicked on your e-mails. If you have a large sales force Zoho also offers enterprise options.

Using a CRM will be important to help you manage your deal flow. You don't want to be managing that in a spreadsheet or word processor or on paper. Make the CRM your friend and enter plenty of notes to remind you what your conversation with the customer was about and why you are calling him again (or not). I make it a habit to enter extensive notes, especially after in-person meetings, so that I can remind myself later about what the client cares about, what the opportunity is about, etc.

Communication is the Lubricant

Like guarding your time, communication is one of the pillars of success. While I covered one aspect of it (E-mail tips) earlier in the book I will elaborate on more points here.

Communication is the top skill companies are looking for in an employee. You read that right. It isn't technical skills, it isn't looks, it isn't how you dress, it's communication! Well, luckily for us sales persons are usually better communicators than let's say engineers or scientists or Bertha in Accounting. Am I right? Well, not always. Average sales persons have a tendency to talk too much and talk when it's not necessary. In "The Client" section of the book I will focus on specific tips on how to communicate with clients but here in "The Self" section I want to focus on general communication skills.

Firstly, take a course on public speaking in college or through a seminar. This is extremely important because it will help you structure your thoughts and polish your delivery. This is not only important for sales but important for advancement in any career. I've seen far too many sales people who ramble without structure in client meetings. Secondly, work very hard to remove awkward filler phrases and words from your speech. Filler phrases and words include things like "uhm", "you know", "you know what I mean", "uhh", "as it were", "if you will", "so to speak", "so", etc. Even the word "so" is a filler word used by countless people. Many people start sentences with the word "so" when clearly its usage is superfluous. The word "like" as a filler word is also very common. Removing filler words from your speech takes a lot of work. Here's how you do it: sit with a partner and start talking about anything. The role of your partner is to ring a buzzer or bell or make an audible sound every time you use an awkward filler phrase. In the beginning you will feel helpless as the buzzer sounds every few seconds. But you will see rapid improvement as you practice this exercise regularly until you no longer have fillers in your speech. What's in it for you? Your clients will pay more attention to what you have to say and you will project sophistication and confidence when you speak without fillers.

When it comes to written communication try to be concise and precise. This requires effort. Read that again please. I cannot stand it (and clients can't either) when senior sales persons spend considerable amounts of time writing long e-mails when I already know the client is not going to read it or when a 30 second voicemail would do. Do not use Emojis or emoticons or cute animated gifs in business communication. This might sound like common sense but I ran across a sales guy once who had an animated cowboy in his signature line. Make your subject line clear. Also, an important note on e-mail: don't e-mail people who don't really need to know the information. If some nitwit sent a meaningless e-mail to you and ten others and you absolutely have to respond then respond only to the sender. This sounds like common sense but I see in businesses people replying to all recipients constantly. I've heard from Directors who are really busy who say that it is extremely irritating. If you want to progress in your career minimize e-mail communication altogether. E-mails have led to the demise of many people. Sensitive information, especially, should never be put in an e-mail. If angry or emotional, never write an e-mail. I wish I could simply say "quit e-mail" but of course you need e-mail for convenience and sharing important and relevant information to those who need to know and to provide a communication outlet for clients who would rather communicate via e-mail instead of the phone. For example, I e-mail clients as a follow up to voicemail. I cover this later in the book in the section on voicemails.

Take a business writing course. Let the professor know you want to improve your written communication for the purpose of business. If you have graduated from college already you can still go back and audit a course or take an elective as a post-graduate.

Not many people realize this but what separates the top people in any career ladder and those below them in the corporate ladder is communication. It's a subtle but overlooked point.

Stop Using the Same Stale Adjectives

There is a tendency people have to use the same adjectives for a wide variety of situations. Sales people are not immune. Words like "amazing" and "awesome" are completely over-used. Your product might be amazing and your service might be awesome but there are other words you can use. For e.g. you can use words like remarkable, delightful, thrilling, spectacular, wonderful, astounding, impressive, etc. Learn to use a wide variety of words because everyone says "amazing" and "awesome" and when you use those words your clients may have difficulty perceiving a difference between you and your competitors.

Prioritize or Die

I see sales people with poor time management skills struggle. Even worse is the inability to prioritize. Is it really important to respond to a client right here right now on a service delivery issue that's minor and the client was asking as a "by the way"? As a sales person if your activities at any given moment in the day are not towards furthering a sale or prospecting then you are not prioritizing what's important. Classify all the things you do as a sales person into priority levels A, B, or C. Do "A" priorities first, then "B", and then "C". Some people use quadrants of "Important/Urgent, Important/Not Urgent, Not Important/Urgent, Not Important/Not Urgent." Draw a square box with four square boxes inside with those four categories and put your weekly activities into each of those four quadrants and handle the Important/Urgent issues first. Then ask yourself which one will lead to greater sales (the Important/Not Urgent or the Not Important/Urgent)? Then address that quadrant followed by the next. The last quadrant to address is Not Important/Not Urgent which you should not touch if the other quadrants are still pending your attention. If you can afford an assistant then delegate the Not Important/Urgent and Not Important/Not Urgent quadrants to her. Prioritization is important in sales and in life.

Sense of Urgency and the Illusion of Sales Solipsism

Top sales people have a sense of urgency that permeates their beings. They aren't the passive player in a deal but actively lead themselves and their clients and their companies through the process. They are always on the hunt for the next deal or for growing an account. They are always looking to penetrate an account. They are always looking to compress the sales cycle and move the deal forward. A sense of urgency permeates their work. For e.g. I have a sense of urgency to get this book published so I can move on to my other projects and I realize every day this book is not on the market I'm losing out on potential book sales. Same thing with your sales deals.

I've been astonished at senior sales reps who leave the onus of follow-up on the client saying things like "oh the client will call back" or "clearly he has no need or he would have called me" or "I've already pestered him with voicemails clearly he has no need." When I stepped in and called the client on their cell phone and set up face to face meetings the client said things like "I'm so glad you are here. I get tens of calls from vendors and I hit delete on their voicemails without listening to them. You're not pestering me at all. I've just been so swamped." Despite hearing a polar opposite narration from the client than what the salesperson assumed was the case some sales people still don't get it. So this is a very important take-away – think of how the client perceives you and put yourself in the client's shoes for a minute. I know this because I have been both a sales person and a buyer. The burden and responsibility of leading the sales process is on you, the salesperson, from beginning to end.

The reality is the client is bombarded today by dozens of calls and e-mails. He will often not call you back even if he knows you unless you are front and center in his mind. He might remember a sales rep from your competitor who had more of his "mind share" than you did. You as a sales person need to know that you're not the only lion in the Serengeti and if you're not patrolling your territory with vigor some upstart young buck will take your zebra and your lionesses.

2 THE CLIENT

The client is the second leg of the tripod of sales success. After all if there is no client there is no sale to be made. I use the term "client" interchangeably with "customer." How you deal with the client, what you say, what you don't say, how you say things, when to say things – these are all crucial skills for sales persons to develop. It takes a lot of concerted effort and practice to get it right but it's not rocket science. If you can muster the discipline and time to improve nobody can stop you from sky-rocketing your sales.

One of the masters of marketing, Philip Kotler, remarked: "Marketing is not the art of finding clever ways to dispose of what you make. It is the art of creating genuine customer value." In that same vein as I will have said several times in this book your success is tied to your customer's success. Your success is tied to creating value for your customer.

I will cover both sales in a B2C perspective and a B2B perspective with emphasis on the latter. The first thing to remember in "The Client" is that you as a salesperson have a collaborative relationship with the client with *their long-term success* in mind. The salesperson-client relationship is not adversarial or competitive but (should be) collaborative. You are not gaming the client. You are not tricking the client. You are not trying to throw sand in their eyes. You really should focus on your client's success. If you focus on your own success you will take short cuts or end up humiliating yourself as I mentioned in the section entitled "You are not Inferior in the Buyer-Seller Dynamic."

I emphasize long-term success for a reason. It is a paradigm the sales person must adopt to keep earning residual income and generating recurring revenue. Your long-term success is in alignment with your client's long-term success.

The Client in B2C

If you are a B2B sales person you can skip to the "The Client in B2B" section. In the B2C (business to consumer) context the sales person might be in retail sales helping customers choose the right electronics or gadgets when a customer walks into a big box store. Or it could be an auto-mechanic who you have approached to fix your car.

The auto-mechanic I use for my car is a person I trust and have used for many years. This auto-mechanic is a technician but if you think about it auto-mechanics happen to sell automotive-repair services. The first few times I needed repairs I got competitive quotes from other mechanics and found my mechanic to be on the lower end price-wise. Being the lowest should not be the sole criteria. What made me really stick with him were two things: Firstly, the repairs lasted as he warrantied them. Secondly, he discouraged me from getting repairs on certain occasions by saying things like "well I can fix it now but you don't really need it, the car will run fine without it" or "this needs fixing but you should be able to drive another 20,000 miles without any issues." So my mechanic cared about my long-term success while sacrificing his short-term gains but paradoxically it resulted in his long-term success because I stuck with him as a customer! This example transcends to B2B clients just as much because if you care about your client's long-term success you are actually caring about your own success. The long-term success of buyer and seller is therefore in alignment. Caring about your customer's success is not just a clichéd phrase. It's an axiom in sales.

To illustrate the stages of sales in a B2C context, let's say you are an electronics sales person at a big box store and a customer comes in enquiring about a 4k Ultra HD TV, how does this dance with the customer proceed? Well, you have established the first thing that needed to be established: **customer interest.** At this stage, the customer is called a prospect. A prospect technically turns into a customer upon completion of a sale. Next, upon establishing customer interest, the average sales people default to identifying some 4K Ultra HD TVs and then talking about the various features and benefits. What's the problem with that approach? The first problem is the customer listens and you're talking in what amounts to a mostly one-way monologue. In sales, especially B2B sales, the client should be talking 80% to 90% of the time while you, the sales person, should be talking 10% to 20% of the time. I really mean it! The top sales professionals understand that "telling isn't selling." If you go on and on about how great the Ultra HD TV is and you don't know why the customer wants a TV or how it fits into the big picture then you're missing the boat! The second problem is you don't know why the customer wants the TV and what size TV he wants or what he'll be using the TV for or anything about the customer. The third problem is you don't know which features and benefits of the long list of features are actually of importance to the prospect. So the next proper set of stages, instead of talking about features and benefits immediately, is to find out for what **purpose** the customer is seeking a TV and what his **criteria** for picking a TV are and what his **budget** for the purchase is and what his **timeline** for decision making looks like. Next **show** him the product and explain how it fits into his criteria (this is where you can mention features and benefits and emphasize those that are of interest to the client). All the while you will be looking for **upsell** opportunities. The final stage is **asking for the sale.**

So let's go over the steps again:

1. Customer Interest: For all intents and purposes this is a binary choice even though you could argue it's more of a Likert scale. The prospect is either interested in something in your store or is not. Usually a sales person elicits an answer to that by asking "Hello Sir, can I help you find something today?" If the prospect responds "no" then say "No worries, just let me know if you need help." If the prospect says "yes" you ask what they are seeking. Let's say they identify a 4K Ultra HD TV.
2. Purpose: Instead of taking the prospect to the section of the store and rattling off features and benefits of random 4K TVs find out why they are seeking a TV as you walk with them towards the TV section. Questions like "Is this for yourself?" can elicit valuable information like whether it's a gift or intended to watch sports or just a family room TV, etc. Let's say he tells you it's for himself and it's to watch sports. You now are able to narrow down specific TVs by asking what dimensions he was thinking of and the size of the room where he wants to place the TV and type of resolution he likes, etc. Now, as soon as he said TV, I'm thinking of upsell opportunities like high performance speakers, TV stand,

warranty for peace of mind, and a great recliner set that would match the aesthetics of the TV and is good for watching sports on with friends. The prospect may not want any of that but you can and should always bring up upsell opportunities if you think it will add value to his TV watching experience. Don't think of the product you are pushing but instead think of the value you are adding to the prospect's life.

3. Criteria: Typically consumers who are purchasing commoditized products like TVs will have one main criterion in mind: price. I discussed this earlier in the book on what types of products are commoditized. Make sure you ask the client: "Sir, what's important to you in addition to the quality of the TV in your buying decision?" He might say price, delivery fees, same-day delivery (no back orders), etc. Once you have the criteria move on to the budget.

4. Budget: Ask the customer if there is a specific budget under which he needs to be and explain that this will help you narrow down the choice of TVs.

5. Timeline: Ask if he's looking to purchase soon or much later in the future and explain that the reason you are asking is because prices change with time. You are also uncovering how serious the prospect is about buying today. For all these stages make sure you ask these questions in an almost nonchalant and casual way. Otherwise the customer will sense high-pressure tactics and balk.

6. Show: I don't literally mean you have to wait till this stage to show him any TV. What I mean is don't start talking about features until this stage because once you know his criteria and budget you have a huge advantage in helping the prospect select the right TV and mention

features he really cares about. If the customer likes what he sees and hears mention casually some upsell products that might complement the TV (like a TV stand, or if he likes games find him some games, etc.) Upselling is huge and can have a material impact on your income and sales. Don't underestimate it. Amazon and Netflix have their versions of upselling called "You might also like..." Also, in addition to showing him selections with his budget you want to show him one or two that are just outside his budget and see if he is flexible. If you do this you will find out that a certain percentage of customers are actually willing to go higher than their stated budget if they really like the product. That's more money in your pocket.
7. Ask for the Sale: I cannot tell you how many sales people do not ask for the sale! Even sales people selling sophisticated financial products or complex software forget to or are too daunted to ask for the sale. If you ask you will double or triple your sale. I am serious! In the TV context you could say something like "So can I ring this order up for you at register 6?"

Dealing with objections is something with which sales people will have to become proficient. In the case of the TV, I already know price will be a key objection because people are living in a knowledge economy and customers have access to information at the tip of their fingers. Guess what? If you sense a pricing objection, say it! You can pre-emptively deal with the objection and say "Mr. Customer, just between you and me, this TV is also available at XYZ Retail Store and Amazon. If you buy it today, I can get it to you for whatever the lowest price is on the market and I'll slap a 5% discount off that lowest price. Just don't tell my boss I told you so."

These types of gimmicks sound canned but in the B2C space

they can and do work. You can even open the latest price comparison app on your phone and pull up that same TV and show the customer that your price is the lowest. This "lowest price" guarantee to close a sale should really be employed if your product or service is commoditized. Otherwise you want to always have a value discussion which I'll cover in the B2B section.

Other gimmicks that work in B2C are also based on similar consumer psychology – e.g. "this is the last TV in stock" (limited supply pressure) or "today is the last day you can get it at this price" (deadline pressure) or "don't tell anyone I'm giving it to you for this price or I might get in trouble" (secrecy and exclusivity gimmick). Personally I don't use gimmicks because I don't sell commoditized products and services and I don't say anything to the client that isn't based at its core in honesty and true value exchange. If you are a B2C sales person I would encourage you to read the B2B section as well because you'll pick up many good tips there as well.

The Client in B2B

In B2B sales you are a salesperson working for a business selling their product or service to another business. Unlike B2C sales you usually won't have customers walking in to look at your products. Your sales cycles (period from customer interest to closure) are much longer than in B2C sales where a sale might close in a matter of minutes. Also, whereas in B2C sales clients are using their own money B2B buyers are using company money to make purchases. There are many more differences which I will mention as we progress.

In B2B sales you will either be an inside sales person making tons of outbound calls to try to find potential customers or you'll be an outside sales person who is customer-facing and visiting clients onsite (at the client's place of business). Inside sales reps sometimes work in conjunction with outside sales reps on the same account (account is a term synonymous with company or client). Some companies just have one type or the other. Inside sales reps work virtually and over the telephone while outside sales reps typically travel to customer sites. Regardless, the first step is still the same where the sales person is trying to reach someone who is a potential customer. This usually takes the form of outbound sales calls. In the initial sales call you are trying to determine three things. Firstly, is the person you are calling the right person to approach about your product or service - in other words confirming their decision making status (or lack thereof). Secondly, you are trying to determine if there is some interest in your product or service. Thirdly, if there is some interest you will ask for a face-to-face (F2F) or virtual meeting to see if there might be a potential sale.

Qualifying Prospects

Now how do you know that Jill (random prospect you are about to call) is the right person to call in the first place? When I started out in sales my sales manager told me to call using whatever lists I could find myself whether it was yellow pages or Yahoo lists or whatever. It was a very inefficient way of doing things and what I call a scatter-shot approach. It's kind of like billboards to a museum exhibit when 90% of the drivers passing by the billboard are not the right audience for that advertisement. You can get a sense of the problem. If you are a Caterpillar heavy duty machinery sales person do you want to randomly call whomever including a retired grandma and the owner of a lawnmower business?

As I grew more experienced I figured out ways to narrow down a list of appropriate potential decision makers. You can get it in one of four ways.

First method: Your marketing department gives you lists to call because they've done their research on the market and who the potential buyers might be. Not many businesses have that luxury of marketing departments performing marketing analytics to determine best candidates.

Second method: You have an insides-sales team or third-party appointment setting vendor (like leadgeneration dot com or Intelliverse) that makes tons of calls for you and passes on qualified decision makers to you or even sets up appointments for you.

Third method: At the end of each day you do your research on a list of people to call the next day. LinkedIn Sales Navigator or just LinkedIn free edition are great sources to mine for prospects. LinkedIn will choke you out after a few searches a day in the free edition by not showing all the information about prospects you are looking up. The way to circumvent that restriction is to always use Google to search and then click on the LinkedIn result rather than doing the search inside LinkedIn's search box. Alternatively, you can pay for a LinkedIn Sales Navigator subscription and perform unlimited searches designed to find prospects. LinkedIn's team of clever data scientists have "productized" the data and have figured out that sales people and recruiters are constantly using the site and therefore they have made it easy for you to find the information you are seeking.

On LinkedIn a good percentage of prospects write intimate details of their role and their business – it's simply mind boggling. They might list how many people report to them, how much their budget is, what key projects they are working on, and many valuable nuggets of information. Always make a note of copying the contact's LinkedIn profile URL into your CRM for easy access to that person's profile later. Or you can copy-paste a description of their key responsibilities so you can refresh your mind every time you call them. Some CRMs like Salesforce even integrate with LinkedIn Sales Navigator.

Based on the third method your initial sales call will morph into something very specific and relatable to the client. Instead of "Are you the person that makes AccountingSoftware purchase decisions?" you might pick a project the prospect has listed on her LinkedIn profile that she's involved with and say "I was calling to discuss key project such-and-such for 2017 and how we have helped clients in your situation with excellent results. Do you have a minute?"

You might be skeptical about the third method but I have closed so many deals using LinkedIn and making targeted initial calls.

Fourth method: Buy a targeted list of contacts. I cover that a few sections later in "Should I Buy Lists?"

Initial Call or the Dreaded Cold Call

Let's go over how this might go in an initial call. Let's say your product is Accounting software (or whatever it is, doesn't matter).

Salesperson: Hi Jill, this is John with AccountingSoftware Company. Do you have a minute? (A variation of this opening could be: Hi Jill, this is John with AccountingSoftware Company. I was calling to explore whether our companies should be working together. Did you have a couple of minutes?)
Jill: (She might respond in many ways including) – 1. Not right now 2. Yes 3. Who are you with again? 4. How can I help you? 5. I'm not interested 6. Take me off your list.
Salesperson: (If she responds with # 1): I'm sorry, when would

be a good time to chat? (Then follow up at that time)
(If she responds with #5 or # 6): Sorry to bother you. I won't be calling you again. Out of curiosity would you know who makes decisions related to Accounting software purchases in your company?
(If she responds with #2 or #3 or #4): Jill, again I'm with AccountingSoftware company. We have been successful at helping Accounting departments like yours improve productivity and smoother tax reporting and I was wondering if you are the person who makes decisions related to software purchases, or upgrades.
Jill: (She might respond with 1. Yes 2. No)
Salesperson: If she responds with "no" say: "Would you know who handles that area?" If she responds with a "yes" say: Wonderful. What accounting software do you currently use and what are some things you wish you could do in your current system that you are unable to do?
Jill: XYZ
Salesperson: Ah, I've had some clients that have used XYZ in the past. Would you have some time for me to drop by and show you how our software is different and how much time it could potentially save you over your current system? (If you are a virtual/inside sales person you would ask for a virtual meeting (like GoToMeeting where you can demo your product and get to know the customer)
Jill: Sure.
Salesperson: How about Jan 7th at 10:00 am? (or ask her for a specific date/time slot that works for her)
Jill: That's fine.
Salesperson: Great. I'll send you a calendar invite shortly and look forward to meeting you. Can you think of inviting any other interested parties to the meeting?
Jill: Yeah, I think I'll invite a couple of more people.

Pointer: If you are a virtual sales person and can do the demo then and there then do so! Compress your sales cycle.

What if the prospect is not interested in AccountingSoftware products? Well then ask her what does interest her and see if there's a match with your services. If you find out that it's a complete dead end thank them for their time and get a referral i.e. ask "can you think of anyone else among your colleagues or business network that might find our services useful?" Don't underestimate referrals. They make a significant impact on your sales. Referrals should be asked regardless of whether you are going to do business with the prospect or not and follow up with: "Thanks for referring me to Joanna. Do you mind if I mention you referred me to her?" If you get that buy-in it will make the reception from Joanna easier because it will become a warm call instead of another cold call.

As a salesperson, the conversation I outlined above where you were able to secure a meeting with Jill would have been a good case scenario where you were able to complete the objectives of confirming decision-making status, interest, and obtaining a meeting. If you are a B2B salesperson who has a large geographic territory you might set up virtual meetings (for e.g. through GoToMeeting) instead of F2F meetings unless your job requires you to travel. Whatever the case, you attained your objective for an initial sales call.

Most of the initial calls will be rejections or voicemails. Don't worry or fret about it and don't take it personally. I faced thousands of rejections in my first year in sales. There was no glimmer of light until finally somebody said "yes" and everything was alright. Some of the calls will be a variation of the conversation above. You might have Jill say she's not the right decision maker but "Jerry Smith handles that" or "I don't make decisions regarding such purchases and I'm not sure who does" or some form of response that takes you back to square one. Just remember, for every few dozen rejections you'll come across a positive outcome that leads to a meeting or some interest. That's what you're looking for and you don't want to be spinning your wheels with people who are not the right fit for your product or service. Your sales manager will have some guidance as to what ratio of calls should lead to a meeting based on averages for the company's sales reps. This ratio varies from company to company and product to product. Your aim is to be the best in your company.

Voicemails, E-mails, or Texts? Tricks of the Trade

First rule of voicemails is to keep it under 20 seconds. Most calls you make will result in the prospect not picking up the phone and you being routed to their voicemail. Should you leave a voicemail and if so what should you say?

Generally speaking, you should leave a voicemail if it's a cold call. You say something similar to what you would say in the initial sales call except that you end it with a call-to-action, that is, you leave your phone number and ask for a call back to discuss further (discuss what further? Your product or a key project they are involved in or whatever is relevant to hook them in or generate interest).

If it's a warm call, mention who referred you and the purpose of your call and end with a call to action. For warm call voicemails mention within the first few seconds who referred you because that's your hook and will prevent the prospect from hitting delete. You would say: "Hi John, this is Joanna from ABC Company and I was referred to you by Bill Perkins in Finance. I was hoping to get a minute of your time to discuss Project XYZ and how we might be able to add value towards a successful completion. Please call me at 123-444-5555 at your earliest convenience. Alternatively, feel free to e-mail me back with a preferred date/time that works for you." That's a 19 second voicemail and under your guideline 20 seconds.

If it's a call to a person you are currently talking to on a deal or who has already expressed some interest in your service or you have done business with in the past then should you leave a voicemail every time you call? There is a variety of opinions here. Some recommend leaving voicemails every alternate call or spacing out voicemails further. Those who pursue the school of thought that you should not always leave voicemails to such customers have to deal with the loss of time issue.

Let me elaborate. I have seen sales people who leave notes in CRM activity after activity saying "Client did not answer, did not leave voicemail." From the salesperson's perspective he has been diligently following up with the client month after month. From the client's perspective nothing at all has happened. He does not know the sales person called him, he does not hear your company's name, he does not hear about your service. Total radio silence. I take the client's side here and say nothing has happened. If you accumulate all these activities where the salesperson has a note which says "called client, client did not answer, did not leave voicemail" this is a significant percentage of time of the salesperson in any given year where he was just a hamster on a wheel thinking he was traveling far distances. So I am not a proponent of the practice of not leaving voicemail (in general). In other words, if you call and get voicemail you should leave a voicemail. The common protest is "but I just called the guy the other week. I'm pestering him." My response to that is "so what if you called him the other week? There is a purpose for the call and that is to establish if this is moving forward or not." One way out of this dilemma is to ask the client every time you do talk to him as to when would be appropriate to follow up. This way you have their buy-in. What if you haven't spoken with them? Then not leaving a voicemail is not helping your cause as a salesperson. It is only prolonging your sales cycle. It is only prolonging the time to qualify your prospect.

Most people do not respond to voicemails. So you give them another outlet to respond to you: e-mails. That's right. After every voicemail I would also send a quick one-line e-mail as a follow up. A lot of people who never bothered to respond to my voicemails actually responded to my e-mails stating they got my voicemail and then they volunteer information that helps me move the sale forward or move off the customer entirely if there is total lack of interest. So moral of the story here is couple your voicemails with e-mails if you want to increase the response rate.

What if neither works? Unbelievably, texting a client on their cell phone gets me the highest response rate. So send them a quick text and you'll get a quick response. Same goes for calls with clients – if you can't get them to pick up their work line call their cell. The pick-up rate is so much higher when I call their cell phone and 95% of clients don't mind if you call them on their cell. Most sales people don't do this and I instantly increase my success rate with these bold moves.

The Dump Message

A tried and tested tool is the "dump message." Use your own variation but it goes something along the lines of: "Hello Jill, this is John Smith from ABC Crate & Barrel Company. I was calling to follow up on your interest in purchasing our custom-sized crates. I've left a couple of messages but have yet to hear back. I'm sure you're very busy and I don't want to bother you with calls that you have no time to return. So this will be my last message. If you're still interested please call me at 123-456-8888. Otherwise I'll assume you are no longer interested or have other priorities and will inactivate your file. Feel free to call me if the situation changes."

Sales people who use the dump message can testify to its success. I'm not a shrink but there's probably something psychologically hurtful about being "inactivated" or not being needed (or treasured). I cannot tell you the number of times a client would not call me until a dump message. The magic of it is that you're being respectful of the client and your own time and getting serious about whether there should be a dance or not.

Word of caution: use your brains and discretion when using the dump message. Do not use it on current customers or customers who have bought from you before or on deals where you know the sales cycle is long or you know the client has already told you the timeline for purchase is 2 years out. Mitigating circumstances should mitigate your usage of the dump message. For current clients who are giving you the run around you can use a variation called the "soft dump message" where you are not inactivating them but using a modified version of the dump message and inactivating the specific opportunity you were discussing.

Personal Cell Phone Numbers are Gold

Sales people usually put in the customer's work phone number in the CRM but very few ask for or put in the client's personal cell phones in CRM. I cannot begin to tell you the value of this step. I have gotten some of the most useful information from clients who had left their previous place of employment and opened up with insightful information and contact names after they left a job. Not only that, you are able to maintain continuity of relationships with a contact into their new place of employment. Guess who has a step up to win the business with a new account that your client just joined from a previous place of employment? You! Make it a habit to always jot down customers' personal cell phone numbers. You might say "well that's awkward asking for a personal cell." Not really. In my two decades of experience only one person asked me why I needed it and I explained that it was to maintain continuity of relationship and how I've even been able to help clients who were transitioning into new jobs. Conversely, I've seen many experienced sales people who could not continue a relationship with a good client because their favorite contact in an account quit and they could not trace him to his new place of employment or get valuable information on successors just when the client quit.

Birthdays and Thank You

If you can find out your client's birthday then send them a birthday card. If not, always send them a "Thank you" card after you conclude a deal. Send them cards wishing them a happy new year. These frequent high-touch gestures of good will go a long way to sustaining a long-term relationship. If you're in B2C and the number of customers is very high then your CRM or e-mail might be leveraged in a cost-effective and time-efficient manner.

For B2B customers, if you have less than 150 contacts you do business with then handwriting them out with physical cards is worth it. I go one step beyond that and write "Thank You" cards to everyone who has been kind enough to allow an in-person meeting.

Should I buy Lists?

This is a question a lot of companies ask. Should they buy lists for their sales people to call? The answer is based on the return on investment. Is it costing too much time now for sales people to find the right prospects? The word "too much" is subjective so you have to break it down to minutes per day and add opportunity cost and then have a dollar figure in hand to compare with the price of a list. But that's not all folks. The efficacy of the list is a huge factor. A lot of companies make tons of money selling lists. Some of them are out-of-date lists where you figure out within a few calls that they haven't refreshed the list in 10 years. Some promise that they refresh their lists every three months but you find examples of contacts that haven't been with the company for 3 years. So there is a lot of variation in the quality of lists. If you ever buy a list make sure you get a money-back guarantee in writing. For example, the seller should state "I guarantee that at least 90% of the contacts in our list are current." If they hesitate you know they are unsure of the quality of the list themselves.

What I personally look for in lists is the one key thing that totally cuts down my time and is very time consuming to obtain by oneself and that is direct dial numbers. Most lists will only have numbers to the main line or switchboard. Direct dials increase your success rate tremendously. There are list companies like DiscoverOrg which have dozens of reps that call prospects to find out their role and keep a regularly refreshed list of working e-mail addresses and direct dials. Such direct dial lists are a dream for seasoned sales reps. Companies like DiscoverOrg go one step further and offer a platform that integrates sales intelligence to their lists – things like what projects the clients are currently working on, what bids are out there in the market from specific contacts, dynamic organizational charts, and more useful information that makes it easy to reach decision makers.

Warm Calls

What I outlined in the initial sales call is called a cold call – something most sales people cannot stand because of the number of rejections. But until you have established your client base you just have to wade through it. I went through that phase heavily in my first year and it was necessary and it helped me polish my phone delivery. My situation was basically the worst case scenario in that I was given no lists and started with zero accounts. My CRM was literally empty. You might join a company and be given some accounts or leads and end up making more warm calls as a proportion of all your calls.

The success rate of warm calls is much higher. A warm call is one that you make to a new prospect but through a link. In other words, it could be something like this: "Hi Jill, this is John from ABC Heavy Industrial Machines Company. I was referred to you by Greg Barnes with whom I had done business before. Do you have a minute?" or it could be something like: "Hi Jill, this is John from ABC Consulting Company. We've worked with several employees at your organization during the past 12 months helping them with key project deliverables and I was wondering if I could schedule a brief meeting with you next week to see how I might be able to help your team as well."

As you read through the scripts in this book just remember that I personally don't use scripts because they are too rigid and mechanical. You have to morph the conversation on the fly but just keep your objectives for each call in mind. Your key objective is to meet your sales goal while caring for the long term success of your client. Every single interaction with a client is in the aim of furthering that key objective. If you deviate from the objective you will struggle.

Know the Trident

The next step after the initial sales call is preparing for a meeting (or presentation as some people call this stage). I don't like the term 'presentation' because it connotes a one-way street where you talk and the client listens. A meeting is a more suitable term because you're establishing a dialogue. But before the meeting I want to take a detour to something that's crucial to your success if you want to become an elite salesperson. Know the trident of your company, your customer's company, and your competitors.

By knowing your company I mean you need to understand why your company exists in the broader economy at all. In other words, what value is your company's product or service adding to the customers? Can the customers do without it? Do you know the full range of products and services your company offers? If not, you will not be able to upsell or cross sell or cross pollinate. You must know your products and services inside-out in your sleep like the back and front of your hand. You must know its strengths and weaknesses and the critical "why should the customer give a darn about my product?" acid test.

By knowing your customer's company I mean you need to be knowledgeable about your customer's company and its operations. If you are going to a Fortune 500 hydrocarbon pipeline company then find out why does the economy even need pipelines? Who are their competitors? What type of revenue and profits do they generate? How do they charge their customers? Are they like a tollway where their customers pay per use? Or is it dependent on the price of the hydrocarbon and therefore susceptible to market swings? Who started the company and when? Now telescope in and ask yourself what does my prospect do exactly in this company and how is their work adding value to the mission of their company to transport hydrocarbons? Please don't be like an average sales person and ask the customer what they do. Know what they do better than they know it themselves. This knowledge will come out in conversation and your client will be super-impressed and immediately trust you. The barriers and resistance to you will naturally melt away. I know this because it has worked for me. But it's not because I want to sell them something and "hit and run". It's because I want to know how I can truly add value to my clients and foster a genuine long-term win-win relationship. Such a bond with your client will ensure that your customer will not even want to consider another vendor as long as you maintain your service levels as promised. I will cover how to "know your customer" in the next section on meetings.

By knowing your competitors I mean know who your top five competitors are and what their products' strengths and weaknesses are. During the decision making process a client will consult with internal stakeholders and assess your bid compared to your competitors. If you know who the competitors are you can act like an internal stakeholder and let the client know how your product is most appropriate for them. Do you want them to bring up the weaknesses and strengths of your product and your competitors' products behind closed doors without you there or do you want to bring that conversation to them yourself with them there? If your answer is the latter you understand that you have a leg up on the competition by acting as an internal stakeholder. Sometimes your competitors are your own client (yes!) because they can do the project internally. Sometimes your competitor is a nifty substitute. For example, if your company crafted an expensive high-tech pen that can write upside down in space (not that there is an "upside down" in space technically speaking) but guess who can beat you at a much cheaper price? That's right, a pencil! Be aware of all your competitors and you'll have a leg up on closing deals.

Preparing for the Meeting

After you've secured a meeting you must prepare for it. If you "know the trident" and prepare for the meeting you will increase your chance of a win and you will be more prepared in meetings than 99 out of every 100 sales person. I have captained sports teams all my life and I don't like going into a match leading my team without knowing the venue, the quality of the grass, the make-up of my opponent, the weather conditions, particular defense weaknesses my team can breach, etc. Same thing applies with meetings with clients. You want to be fully prepared. Your clients will appreciate it too because instead of facing them as opponents you are joining them as a strong and fully prepared extension of their team. I usually take 10 to 15 minutes to prepare for a meeting the day before a meeting. Here are things I look up:

- Read the LinkedIn profiles of all the attendees to find out what key projects they are involved in and what roles they play.
- Skim through the client company's website to find out what products/services they sell.
- If they are a public company, I download and skim through their 10-K report from the Investors section of their website to find out how profitable they have been the last 3 to 5 years, whether they have positive operating cash flow, who their key customers are, what

their main challenges or goals are (you don't have to read through the entire 10-K to obtain this information. It's usually sectioned in the table of contents as "Financial Statements" and "Management Discussion & Analysis").
- Do a loose match in your mind of how your set of products/services might fit into or add value to their company based on what you read in their 10-K. By the time I have read through their 10-K I usually know more about their company than the prospect (from a high level perspective).
- Read Account notes in CRM to see who else you've done business with in the account so you can casually name drop during the meeting. This establishes credibility and trust.

I do all this in 10 to 15 minutes or less and with practice you can as well. Initially it might take you an hour to do all the above steps but force yourself to get the time down to 10 minutes.

The Meeting

The very first client meeting I had was a total wreck. I did not follow methodology. I was stammering. I was talking most of the time. I was anxious. It was a blur and a nightmare. It was first time jitters. The client was actually very kind and based on my relatively young age realized I was inexperienced. My boss didn't know what happened and I kept mum about it. But I did not quit. The second meeting I had was much better and I was able to close a deal in my very first month in sales and exceed quota even though I knew absolutely nothing about sales when I joined and had zero accounts to my name. So if you have had a bad meeting or if you are nervous initially don't worry – you'll get over it very quickly. However, it took me a while to learn the art and finesse of a meeting.

Whether you are meeting the client virtually or in person the objectives are the same. Your objectives are to accomplish as many of the following as possible:
- Uncover client needs to see if there is a match with your services or products.
- Suggest to them things they haven't even considered that might be of help to them.
- Get a referral to others in the organization that might benefit from your services or products.
- If there is a potential match then flesh out the opportunity right there or set a follow up meeting/time to discuss details if the timing of the meeting is pre-mature. (More on how to flesh out an opportunity in the section entitled "The Opportunity (or Potential)."

For complex high-dollar deals I always prefer meeting in person because you can gauge the client's reactions and read in between the lines much better through non-verbal communication. Most of communication is non-verbal. Body language, facial cues, tone, pitch, and even intent are much easier to interpret in person. Also, a client remembers you much better if you have met them in person and you stand out from among the 20 other sales reps from other companies that have also been calling her.

If you are meeting in person be well-groomed, have a confident erect posture (don't slouch) and be relaxed. Dress well – I personally don't like wearing ties as I feel it constricts oxygen-rich blood that my brain most needs in a meeting but I will wear a jacket and pressed attire with decent shoes. Be there at the client site around 5 to 10 minutes prior so you can check in, get your badge, and be escorted to the client's office or a conference room. If offered beverages it's better to decline politely and thank them for asking unless you're there for a marathon meeting. Never be late to a meeting. That will project unreliability and reduce your chances of doing business.

The most important thing to remember is that in an initial meeting (and most meetings really) the client should be talking 80% of the time or more and the sales person should be talking 20% of the time or less. It's an easy rule on paper but hard to implement. But I guarantee you that once you implement this rule you will see your sales increase. The problem is that most sales people take refuge in talking about their products and services and just go on and on thinking that telling is selling. The customers over the years have become accustomed to this dog and pony show type of presentation where the sales person is all agog about their service and inside the client starts yawning or making judgment calls on whether the product or service will be of benefit to them. Because of the bad habits of sales people customers automatically start off a meeting asking the salesperson to tell them about their company and products. The sales person then dutifully starts his dog and pony show and leaves the meeting with nothing. If you were a patient in a doctor's office would you ask the doctor, "so tell me about what diseases you can treat?" and the doctor then starts a dog and pony show and spends the next 20 minutes narrating his credentials and what illnesses he can treat? What about if you went to a grocery and you asked the grocer "so tell me about what grocery items you sell here?" and the grocer then starts a dog and pony show about the 1,000 products he carries in his store? To me, when a client starts off a meeting asking me to tell them about my company and products, it is just as absurd.

You have to pre-emptively direct (and constantly re-direct) the client to why you're really there – to help them help you help them! You have to constantly monitor the 80-20 speaking ratio during the meeting. Here is what you say when you show up at the meeting: "Jill, thank you so much for having me over today. I know we have limited time so to make our meeting as productive as possible I want to ensure we cover only things that are pertinent to you and key projects you are overseeing. Do you mind if we start with your top priorities and challenges?" This opening line is worth memorizing because otherwise you'll get caught flat footed doing a dog and pony show. The only modification I have to that opener is if you've done business with other contacts in the account then mention briefly that you've worked with their colleagues to help them achieve their project goals.

The key is to keep the client talking and keep things open-ended. Get out all the issues that a client is facing even if initially it does not seem like there is a match to your services. When the client seems to stop, make a statement like "I've come across these types of issues with some of our other clients" and then keep the faucet of information flowing by asking "what else can you think of that pose significant challenges?" You need to keep asking the "what else" question because I've come across crucial challenges that clients mention only towards the end because they don't want to discuss the most intransigent challenges right off the bat. Those are also where some of your biggest opportunities will pop up. So don't tire of asking "what else?"

When the client points to problems ask them "how do you know it is a problem?" and "what metrics do you use to measure it?" Most sales people don't go deeper and uncover the multi-layered richness that is inherent in client challenges. It's in the deeper layers where you'll uncover a lot of your high-dollar opportunities. If they aren't measuring the problem's impact they cannot improve it but you can help. What's the point of asking "how do you know it is a problem?" You ask this to figure out if this is the real problem or a symptom of a deeper underlying problem. I've found that clients who are gently guided through a series of probing questions eventually open up and find the process cathartic as if I'm a corporate mediator or counselor. Importantly, it gives me deep insight into all the issues and how my company might (or might not) be able to solve their issues.

If the client insists on the old dog and pony show and does not tell you anything until you've started sharing something about your company and its products then have a very brief 20 second value proposition statement and re-direct back to the client. I know some technical sales guys will protest right now and say "my product's technical specifications and details are highly relevant and I need to discuss these in-depth with my client." My answer to that is "Fine, but just not right now." Wait until the client has revealed all the issues because if you rush it you won't be able to upsell or cross-sell and you will cost yourself money and you won't be serving the client to the best of your abilities.

It is really important that you know your company's value proposition statement. Ask your boss and make sure it takes only a few seconds to clearly articulate your value proposition. I go on so many technology websites these days where I just cannot figure out the value proposition. It's a mess! You should know your value proposition which is a statement of why a prospect should pay attention to your product and a compelling reason they should consider buying it from you. Once you've made a value proposition statement like "Our company cuts down the time for BOP re-certifications by 30% over the standard re-cert times saving our clients an average of $20 million in lost production" you can re-direct and say "We perform a lot of ancillary services that might help you. Can you share some of your ongoing challenges around BOP re-certifications so I can focus on where we could most add value to your company?" By the way, I just made up that value proposition and those numbers. The point here is you should have a short but clear value proposition and then re-direct the client back to their issues! Forget the dog and pony show.

If I can offer a simpler analogy on not rushing things, it is like a customer who comes into an office supply store asking for paper and the average sales person directs them to the paper aisle but an above average sales person walks them to the aisle and asks what they are using the paper for and oh by the way did the customer know that the store offers loyalty discounts and the cheapest toner cartridges in town and can print business cards for your sales staff and print and post flyers? Instead of an $8 transaction an above average sales person might get a lifetime value of hundreds of dollars out of this customer by simply getting all the issues out.

Getting back to the meeting you will at this point know if there is an opportunity where your company can help. Once you establish an opportunity if the need is imminent you will go through the process of moving the sale forward which I'll describe in the following sections. If the need is not imminent you will set up a follow up meeting at the appropriate time and get referrals and part with pleasantries and agreed upon action items.

Account Penetration

If you get referrals make sure to follow up with them right away. These will be warm calls and you might uncover opportunities with them. Penetrating an account is easier with referrals and you'll have multiple pockets of opportunities with multiple people in multiple departments or teams. I can't tell you how many sales people I have seen who are working on Fortune 1000 accounts where they are doing business with just one or two people. That's insane! That's also minimal account penetration. If you are in services you can potentially be pitching your solutions to many different teams. I have seen major Fortune 10 accounts under the hands of mediocre sales people who were calling the same set of 5 or 10 people and doing business with 1 or 2 of them and they rested on their laurels. The same account when transferred over to an elite sales person just blew up thirty-fold. I mean literally the revenue from the account went up by a multiple of 30. Why? Because the elite sales person got referrals and built on every success and understood that decisions in major corporations are very often de-centralized even when a contact might claim that decisions are centralized. The elite sales person then had sales coming in from multiple departments and multiple teams in multiple countries with a wide variety of services he was matching to the client whereas the mediocre sales person was dealing with a local contact and selling a narrow set of services with which he was comfortable. Part of it is because the sales person was convinced by the claim of the local contact that he was the end all be all master decision maker. Even veteran senior sales reps fall for this claim of centralized power with bewildering naiveté. A contact might claim centralization to hold on to power or because they just aren't aware of other pockets of independent decision making bodies within an organization. Be smart and penetrate an account as much as possible.

If you are selling something extremely specific like an electron microscope then I can understand you won't be able to penetrate an account as much as a services sales person would because your set of decision makers would be limited. The point is know who all your possible decision makers might be and don't rest on just one or two when the set of decision makers is much larger.

The Magic Portfolio

This is a nifty psychological trick I learnt from a top sales person which really worked. He had a leather portfolio (also called a leather binder or padfolio) in which he had the notepad on one side to take notes during a meeting. The other side of the binder had slots for eight business cards which you could see through clear plastic. He would insert business cards of previous people he met and arrange them by company. So if he was visiting, let's say, a new prospect at General Electric, he would have the General Electric (GE) business cards (from his prior meetings) displayed on one page. The client on the other side of the table could glance into the binder and see that the sales person had already met a number of other GE decision makers and this would instantly decrease resistance to talking and increase cooperation and trust. Gather all the business cards and have your own magic binder.

Listening Skills: The Power of the F-Bomb

I still struggle with this one but the cream of the crop sales people work very hard at listening skills. It requires focused concentration and it requires a deliberate intent to actually want to listen to what the client is saying. The mind of the sales person tends to drift to what he is going to say next or what response he has to something the client just said. Don't interrupt the client. Don't check your phone if it buzzes (in fact silence your phones during meetings). Listen and watch the client's facial cues and if you listen deeply you will pick up what's being said between the lines. Getting to that stage of expertise will really serve you well in your career. I think I have met less than five sales people in my whole life who were expert listeners. Practice this with your friend or colleague or partner. First try to listen for a minute with full concentration and then gradually increase that duration until your mind gets into a zone where your focus is 100% on the client.

Listening skills are under-rated by sales people but I've seen egregious examples of senior sales reps completely misunderstanding or not hearing key opportunities that were being uttered by the client. I've been in meetings where the client mentioned the names of three other colleagues and what they were in charge of and the sales person who was furiously writing down notes missed all that information. This was because they were distracted by internal thoughts on what to say next or they were de-valuing their customer's speech or because they hadn't worked at cultivating great listening skills. This is a costly mistake. Make sure you work really hard on mastering listening skills. The F-bomb (focus) is the key to listening and a key weapon in your arsenal. If you improve your listening skills it will have a dramatic impact on your sales.

Empathy

I alluded to this earlier in the book but sales people are not very good at empathizing with clients. The primary reason is because they haven't been on the other side. As Harper Lee's character in "To Kill a Mockingbird" said "You never really understand a person until you consider things from his point of view…until you climb into his skin and walk around in it."

The client is another human being with a career and bills to pay. They have the same emotional strengths and frailties as you. But also realize the client today is extremely busy. They deal with 100+ emails a day and sometimes a dozen calls in a week from sales people. They cannot remember you from the next sales person. If he rejects you and is curt it's because you're the seventh guy that interrupted his project today and by the way his boss is stepping on his throat to meet an impossible deadline. Also, they just went through a layoff of 3,000 workers so everyone is jittery. Or they just had a growth spurt and he got passed over for promotion and he's not too happy. The sales person needs to keep all that in mind and make it very easy for the client to do business with him.

The Client is not your Friend

I don't understand sales people who sight unseen make personal comments about their mortgage or marital status or child support payments or drone on and on about the weather and hair loss or weight gain or whatever. The client does not need to know if you live on the west side with silver cutlery or you take a bus to work out of the projects. Don't share anything about your personal life where the client might make a judgment call that may go against you. You can be very friendly with a client without being a friend. I've also seen sales people who befriend clients and then feel like they should not "sell them" anything as if they were pushing crack and are now saving their friends from it. It's totally preposterous. You can share a laugh with a client and genuinely care about your client's success without befriending them. I've seen over the years that sales people who have friends in client accounts end up selling those people nothing. Nor are they the great fountains of information that they are purported to be. Whereas those with whom they maintain a friendly, respectful, polished, and professional relationship, the fruits of such unions are beneficial to both parties.

An exception - in certain cultures being a friend is a pre-requisite to doing business. You eat, drink, laugh, make merry, even visit each other's houses and then sit down to talk about business. So know your context and culture.

Connect the Dots and Show Them the Way

Connecting the dots is not simply about matching your services and products to your client's needs. It is about looking for patterns in the whole ecosystem that surrounds your client in terms of personnel, projects, needs, priorities, goals, hurdles, etc. You must often take a step back after telescoping down to an individual contact's needs and see how it all fits into the larger picture. I personally always look at how the particular contact I'm dealing with plays a role in their company and how the current opportunity I am working on with the client fits into objectives stated in the company's 10-K. I also look at how their project meshes in or diverges from other projects with other contacts in the same account. Often the client contact themselves won't see the big picture because departments and functional units are often in silos and don't talk to one another. You can guide them towards that big picture so that they see you as an extension of their team and not as just a third party vendor. Here are ways the very top sales people add value to the client beyond just matching solutions to expressed needs:

- Understand and empathize with clients and their surroundings. For example, if it's a non-traditional rapidly changing environment with a matrix structure I will explain how other clients in similar situations have faced similar problems and how I have been able to help them successfully navigate uncertainty.
- The client will express certain needs to you if they trust you. But if you fulfill those needs will it make their problems go

away? Is there something else you could add that might add value that they aren't even thinking about? Write down the client's expressed needs and then write down next to those needs all the unexpressed needs you think if addressed would align with the stated objectives in the client's 10-K report. Connect the dots for the client and he will forever see you as a trusted counselor.

- Don't wait till the customer expresses a need. If you heard about two companies merging into one massive behemoth and you know from your reading and studies all the problems that emerge during such mergers then let your client know some of the things they can expect and how you might be able to help him pre-empt them or be ready to face them. Advise him that he should do certain things in such situations to achieve certain outcomes because you have seen it work in XYZ merger.

- Don't just ask the customer how you can get set up on their vendor list. If you are working with a large multi-national which issues hundreds of thousands of purchase orders and has 60,000 vendors you are just another speck of dust. Rather, flip the paradigm and coach the client on how they can buy from you. This might require some investigation on your part but you take that work and excuse off the hand of your customer and ensure that doing business with you is easy.

Know your customers intimately. Know what they buy, why they buy, how they buy, when they buy, and what else they wish they could have bought that you didn't provide and what else you think they ought to consider buying that hasn't even crossed their mind. Completely envelope your clients with your expert counsel if you want to be an elite sales person.

To Lunch or not to Lunch

Asking a client to lunch is appropriate if you have met them or spoken to them before. There is something about a lunch that is viewed as a favor by clients and because clients are generally good human beings they return the favor by offering insight into their work or their company. I have received organizational charts from clients through lunch meetings and tons of referrals and information about key projects that are going on in a company.

Compress the Sales Cycle or I'm okay with a "No"

This goes back to guarding the time and closing more deals. The sales cycle does not have to be one day or one minute longer than it should be. If the prospect you are calling has interest but tells you the right time to call him back is December which is two months out then set an activity to call him on December 1st. I've seen sales people in such scenarios who set an activity to call the client on December 17th or December 12th which is arbitrarily late and completely disrespectful of the salesperson's time. Not to mention that between December 1st and December 17th a competitor's sales person might be getting in while you're sleeping. If the client keeps you at bay or drags deals on it might be because they don't want to hurt your feelings. So give the client the option to say "Yes" or "No" because either way it will save you time. Don't let them keep you in the purgatory land of "Maybe" or "No decision." Clients who say "No" are saving you a lot of time and are being respectful of the realities of the situation. That is to say you arrive mutually to an agreement that there's no real match for your respective companies to be doing a deal. A large majority of sales people don't understand the importance of compressing the sales cycle or eliciting a "Yes" or "No" response as early as possible in the sales process. They will keep the "No" at bay for as long as possible but in the process end up wasting so much time that could have been reassigned to other deals. A sales person might work for weeks on a deal to find out that the client has no money in the budget and he was afraid to bring it up because he wanted to avoid the "No."

A Word on Trade Shows

Depending on your product and how competitive your market is, trade shows or conventions where you have a booth and showcase your service or product might generate solid leads and opportunities and sometimes it might not. You have to be careful with trade shows and attend only those where the visitors are potential decision makers. I've seen sales people who were able to close significant deals from trade show leads and some that got nothing out of it. Usually sales people are not good at following up on trade show leads because they return to work and get busy with their usual calling and prospecting. If you attend a trade show make sure you follow up with the people who dropped by your booth.

Sometimes you would attend a trade show just to keep up with partners, key customers, and competitors. Trade shows give you a chance to see what your competitors are up to and how you are ahead of or behind the curve.

A Word on Commitment

Commitment to your client is closely tied to your credibility. If you commit to a client that you will have something delivered by a certain date or that you will call him by 8:30 am then do so and if for extenuating circumstances you cannot, then call him to apologize and explain why you will have to re-schedule but don't make it a habit. A client might forgive a commitment breakage for extenuating circumstances once or twice but after that they'll look for another provider. When you call to explain your extenuating circumstances don't say something moronic like "John, we've had five people let go last Friday and my operations manager was busy juggling schedules and the big boss is in town so can we re-schedule?" No matter what the excuse is be generic about it and move to the call-to-action right away. Say something like "John, I'm sorry I know we were supposed to have a meeting at 4:00 pm tomorrow but I've got a personal matter that needs my urgent attention. Would you mind if we move the meeting up to today or day after tomorrow at 2:00 pm?" More than likely, your client will understand (as long as it's not a habit of yours to break commitments). Just be generic and professional and do not divulge company secrets or personal secrets thinking your client will sympathize or empathize with you. Maybe he will, maybe he won't. Why take a chance?

There's another level of commitment that I want to mention here. The client should feel like he is the only client you are attending to when you are talking to him. You shouldn't mention how you might miss a pending deadline on a delivery because all of a sudden you had two other client projects dumped on your table and those clients are more important (or even equally important). If you bring up other clients it will just get on your client's nerves and he'll switch to a vendor where he knows he'll get a better (perceived) level of service. I've had clients who flat out said "we like working with small companies because the larger companies have reps that are handling too many clients and we slip through the cracks and we don't get the service level we pay for." The truth is that your handling of other clients is inconsequential to the promise or commitment you made to any given client. So don't make the faux pas of telling your client that his project has to wait because you have other more pressing clients to take care of than him. You made the commitment to do business with him so fulfill your commitment and then later on decide whether you want to do further business with him. But always follow through on any commitment you make. If you're halfway through a project and start waffling on the deliverables not only will you have a pissed off client but it will speak volumes about your lack of commitment and you won't be able to sustain long term clients. This might sound like common sense but I've heard several sales people and consultants who've used other clients as an excuse for poor deliveries or missed deadlines.

A Word on Humor

Not everyone is born with a good sense of humor. I personally am able to make even the most serious executives laugh with well-timed jokes and observations. But not everyone has that innate ability. I have seen sales people who tried cringe-worthy jokes. If you're good at it then leverage it but use it sparingly and by sparingly I mean once or twice in a meeting to break tension or break the ice. You do want to present yourself as a serious businessman with a dignified and powerful presence. If you're constantly joking your services might also be considered a joke.

The Opportunity (or Potential)

If your initial meeting (see the section titled "The Meeting") did not lead to an opportunity then thank the client for their time and part as friends and keep the door open for future business and get referrals on the spot. Often a client who meets you but cannot give you any business for whatever reason will not mind referring you to a colleague whom she thinks might be a better fit.

If your meeting leads to an opportunity you may be able to close it right away (especially true for B2C customers) or it may take a series of additional phone calls or meetings to progress the deal to closure (especially true for B2B customers). How you deal with an opportunity can make or break you. So firstly how do you elicit all the issues out so you know what the opportunities are? I explained some of the methods in the section entitled "The Meeting." Now I will elaborate further.

The key is to probe several layers deep and not be satisfied with statements from clients that require further elaboration. A lot of sales people have trouble with probing because they think it's either rude or they grasp on to the first opportunity they hear and cling to it as if there is no other opportunity. Probing deeply requires following a method with a few key principles:

1. Ask open-ended questions.
2. Don't talk most of the time. You're better off if the client is speaking the majority of the time (even as high as 80% to 90% of the time). This is one of my top three pieces of advice for you to become an elite salesperson. The more you speak the more chances there are that you'll make mistakes, or bore the client, or just fall into pushing product.
3. Listen very carefully to everything the client is saying (and not saying). You will need to do this to connect the dots and look for patterns in the account.
4. Do not dwell too long on what I call surface questions like "how many people work in your team?" or "what software are you currently using?" or "what problems are you currently having?" These are fine to spend time on as an opener but what separates the mediocre sales professionals from the elite are what I call impact questions. The impact questions are magical in that they make the client get into the sales person's shoes as to

why they need to buy your product or service. Examples of impact questions are as follows:

a. Jill, you have identified X, Y, and Z problems/challenges/goals. What effect will solving these problems (or achieving these goals) have on your team's output? What if you do nothing?
b. Jill, we talked about XYZ issue that is really hampering your team's productivity. If you don't do anything to solve this problem and keep to the status quo, how much money will you lose this year?
c. John, we talked about how our re-cert program will get your team up to speed. How will meeting the federal regulations help you and how many dollars in fines can you avoid this year by being up to par?
d. John, given that our printers are 70% faster with the same level of quality as your current printers and at the same cost, how much of your back log of orders will you be able to flush out of the system and how much additional revenue will that bring you this year?

Do you see a pattern in these impact questions? It's turning the job of selling this product and service around to the client! Make them see with their own eyes and ears how much of an impact your solution will have on them. Then, quantify it for them. I repeat, quantify it for them if they don't quantify it for you first. Once you quantify it for them, ask them if they believe that this is a realistic number because I have seen sales people lose deals where after quantifying it a decision maker like a CIO did not go with them because when asked later on by researchers they admitted that they did not believe in the quantified value of the solution.

So answers to the above impact questions could be as

follows:

a. If I solve this problem of lack of training of my coding specialists my attrition rate will reduce by 50% and that's going to save the company $400,000 this year. (Remember, walk them through the quantification and then ask them if that's a conservative estimate and if they believe it)

b. If I don't eliminate this missing information issue in our purchase orders we will continue getting late payments from our main customers. (If they stop here, press the issue to quantify the impact). Ask: And what percentage of your receivables are late because of this issue? Answer: 30%. Ask: And we've seen how our software can eliminate the human middle man and get information flowing both ways to eliminate late payments from your three key customers. How much in interest payments will you save from having to borrow for working capital because of late payments currently? Answer: It's got to be at least $1.5 million a year. Ask: Would you say that's a conservative realistic estimate? Answer: Yes.

Now if your solution is worth $275,000 to solve a $1.5 million a year problem and your competitors aren't solving it equally proficiently for cheaper, then the client has made the sale for you through you guiding them through the impact questions. Most sales people miss the impact questions.

c. Our operations will risk getting shut down and that brings $7 million in profits in California alone. Plus we stand to continue getting fined to the tune of $400,000 a year. (Based on this answer and based on the cost of your solution you can walk them through the impact and get their buy-in to make it much easier to close the deal)

    d. Gosh, I am sure our back log would be completely eliminated by faster printers. (If the client is not sure, you would have a simulation or a demo showing them how each percentage reduction in backlog would result in quantifiable incremental revenue. But by now you've already shown it to him and he knows how much additional revenue there is to gain and you simply confirm whether he believes the number is realistic and then ask for the sale).

Also, if you sense something is off say it! (See the section entitled "If You Sense it Say it" for an elaboration). Top sales people will not hesitate to call a client out (in a polite way) if something seems off. For e.g. "Mr. Client, you have had this problem for five years and have not been able to implement a solution. What's different now?" Here the client might give confirmatory answers or astonishing answers that tell you that you need to move on. Confirmatory answers might include "Well, we have a new CTO and he has made it a top priority to get this resolved this year and he has allocated money towards it whereas previously we had no funding to address the issue."

Another important question to ask is "on a scale of 1 – 10 with 10 being the highest, how important would you say it is for you to get this problem resolved or this goal achieved?" If the answer is a lukewarm 5 or 6 or lower then question the client as to the seriousness and move on if it's not a high priority to them.

Time, Timeline, and Money

In parallel with the opportunity definition you are also going to find out if the client has shoes to dance – meaning it's all well and good if the client knows your solution is a good fit but what if he does not have the money to pay for it nor the time needed to participate in helping a solution be implemented? You will end up doing all this hard work and find out he has no money. So how do you find out if the client has the time and money or not?

Once I was consulting for a company where the sales person was working on an opportunity. As the deal was developing the sales person qualified the money issue early on in the process by asking the client a key question: "John, have you set aside some funds for this project we are discussing?" You can ask this question a number of different ways for e.g. you could ask "John, have you established a budget for a solution to this problem?" or "John, how were you planning to fund this project?" or "John, is this coming out of your annual budget?" etc. However you phrase it you need to bring it up during the opportunity definition. The sales person did not however find out how much money the client had in his budget. This is another crucial "Time and Money" question. So the sales person and his support team was spending a good amount of time writing a proposal and was about to send it in and I told them to hold their horses and get the client on the phone.

As we conference-called the client my objective was to determine how much money the client had and if I could not establish that then I needed to establish if the client would be able to pay for what we were going to price the deal. Here's a shortened version of the call focusing on the money issue.

Me: John, we have an understanding with your team that we will be able to get the deliverables to you by the stated deadline. Were you able to secure approval on the budget? (I re-asked this even though it was established previously)

Client: Yes we can get this funded.

Me: How much were you hoping to get allocated towards this project?

Client: I don't know. You tell me. As long as it's not too high we should be okay. As long as it's not a million dollars! (Now this is one of several responses the client might give including revealing to you the budget or asking you what it should cost or flat out saying that they don't have a budget at all. Note how subjective the term "too high" is)

Me: Well I can assure you it will cost somewhere between $1 and $1,000,000. (Now I said this to break the tension and awkwardness of the money discussion and it caused everyone in the call to laugh)

Client: Well as long as it's under $100,000 I will be able to get it signed off on.

Me: John, thanks for that. We'll get the contract over to you today. Do you think you'll be able to get Nick to sign off on it this week since we are slated to commence the project next Wednesday? (Here you are trying to find out when you are going to close the deal).

The call then proceeded to a discussion on logistics and contract details.

The salesperson and the entire team now knew a crucial bit of information – that to win the deal they had to price it under $100,000 which was well within the profitability margin and actually it allowed us to increase our margins because we knew the cap.

Typically if the client does not give you a budget at all then you have to test them by asking: "Usually in deals like this our clients pay anywhere between $50,000 and $80,000 (or whatever range is within your profitability target as long as the lower number and upper number are somewhat close together – my range of $1 to $1,000,000 is not what you would seriously say but it worked because it was said in jest). Here's what you say: Mr. Client, is that within the range of your budget?

The client might say "yes" in which case you have what you needed or they might say "no." If they say "no" it is one of several reasons:
1. They just don't have any money and were doing a market search to see whether they should do this internally
2. Range is higher than what they had earmarked in the budget in which case you ask if they could accept a trimmed down version of the project deliverables or if they can pay a portion of the project with this year's budget and the remainder next year in the first quarter (or whatever terms your company is okay with)
3. Range is higher than what they think the project is worth or what they think your company's work is worth. Here you go back to the impact questions and quantify the results and test their beliefs and ask for the business after resolving any belief issues.
4. Range is higher than what they believe the market is asking for which typically means you have competitors who price it for lower or the client believes that without any basis in reality. Here you ask the client to sit down and compare your projected results with that of your competitors' results and differentiate between your competitor and yourself. This might be in terms of faster deliverables, higher quality, better reputation, better guarantees or warranties, additional services that are different but that the client had not seen. After differentiating between you and your competitors ask the client if they believe the price difference is worth the difference in project deliverables. If the answer is yes

you still win the deal even if you are priced higher. If the answer is "no" then you offer a trimmed down version of your services at the same price or lose the deal and move on.

If you lose the deal, provide input to your superiors and product / services and marketing people to see if there is something fundamentally stronger in your competitor's products and services that requires your company to re-tool and overhaul that particular product or service line.

If the range is higher because of a false belief that the client has about the market then ask him "and what makes you say that?" and keep probing until you clarify his misconception about the price and upon correction of the false belief you should be able to close the deal. For example, if the client believes a new car is worth only $3,000 this is a false belief and you ask why he believes that. Then help him see the light with market data on what new cars are worth. This belief correction applies just as much to services.

Next, time needs to be addressed in parallel during the opportunity definition phase. By time, I mean if your solution requires your client to allocate their team's time then you need to get their buy-in that they can commit to such time towards the success of the project. If yes, you have cleared that hurdle and if not you ask "I believe we can be successful in achieving the goals you articulated but it does require the commitment of five of your employees for at least 20% of their work week towards this project. How do you suggest we move forward?" Potential solutions are where they pay you more to hire more people to help or where they themselves shift around workers for a period of time to help with the success of the project or they allow you to extend the deliverables date. In other words, something has got to give. Time issues are not applicable to every product or service.

Next, project timeline issues are crucial. You find out that the client needs to get rid of all these disparate IT applications and replace them with an ERP. They want to start to do a feasibility study two years from now and that's a big maybe. If the timeline is not defined and the client will not work with you to pin down a timeline don't waste your time on it. Just follow up when things get closer.

Who is the Shot Caller – the Mistake Every Salesperson Makes

This is an area where the top sales people separate themselves from the mediocre sales person. Most sales people, including many senior sales people, don't want to confirm that the person they are talking to is indeed the shot caller (decision maker). It is rarely the case that the contact you are talking to about a deal is the decision maker or the sole decision maker. If you know who the decision makers are you have a huge leg up on your competitors. One of the reasons for sales people being unwilling to probe into this area is because they feel they would be going around the contact or undermining the contact or being too nosy. Nonsense! If you don't know who the decision makers are you don't know how they will make a decision and you won't have any firm position to win the deal. It is crucial that you find out who are calling the shots and what each of them cares about in the deal. Some might be influencers, some might just provide positive (or negative) critiques but aren't making the decision, some are involved just on the money side (e.g. a Controller), some are there just to rubber stamp the deal, and then some actually have a lot at stake in the deal going through or not going through and some stand to win a lot if the service you provide adds value to their role in the company. Understand, and I mean deeply understand, each decision maker's role in the deal and post-deal. If you do your homework on the shot callers you'll have a much higher chance of winning a deal.

The way to elicit this is through any combination of the following questions:

1. John, now we've defined the problem you are wanting to address. Who does the solution impact in your company?
2. John, obviously you are involved in the decision making process. In order to get this solution adopted and signed off on, who else needs to review the deal and when?
3. John, I know getting this adopted will make a huge difference to your team and I want to make sure you look good throughout the entire process of implementation. But in my experience not everyone in a company has the same level of enthusiasm for a solution as the contacts with whom I'm talking. If I come out there and present this to your team of decision makers and stake holders it would likely make adoption much easier. Would you be able to host a meeting where all the decision makers and stake holders are together so I can address each of them and their concerns?
4. John, I understand you are the final decision maker and your CFO simply has to rubber stamp the deal. Is there anyone else involved who could scuttle the deal or help in getting it passed through?
5. John, besides yourself who else is involved in getting this deal done and dusted? Out of respect for the stakeholders' times do you mind if I talk to them to get their take on what's important to them so that our final presentation will address each of their concerns beforehand?
6. John, I know we discussed the EVP has a stake in getting this deal killed. Who do you think can help us get this adopted despite the resistance from the EVP? How

will your company go about in making a decision on this deal? Can we invite the EVP as well to get his take on things so perhaps we can address his concerns as well or is his take purely political?
7. John, in order to get this deal signed what needs to happen and who needs to get involved with you?

You start to see a pattern in the questions and you start to realize why most sales people are not comfortable asking these kinds of questions. I'm telling you, just trust me, if you follow through in finding out who the decision makers are and what's important to each of them and who has a stake in getting this adopted and who has a stake in getting this killed, you can propose a solution that will blow your competition out of the water and appeal to most, if not all, of the stakeholders. If you know who all the decision makers are and what they each want to see then you will never inadvertently put a square peg in a round hole.

Bypassing Pseudo-Decision Makers

Often you'll run into dead ends with prospects who you think are decision makers but you know from your initial questioning that there are others involved. Many sales people make the mistake of thinking that initial contact is the end all be all and if they go over his head then they might offend him. I routinely "go over" the heads of what I call pseudo-decision makers. These people are more like gate keepers and will not share much information and do not pull the trigger on decisions. You will gain a sense as you grow in sales experience when it is okay to bypass such pseudo-decision makers and reach out to their bosses who call the shots. There are a couple of ways. One default way is when the contact does not return your calls or e-mails so bypassing him should pose no problems. Another way is when the contact is protective and guarding the true decision makers you get his buy-in and ask to meet all of them together so that you provide a solution that makes him look good. Another method is to get someone in your company who is superior to you in the hierarchy to call his bosses. That way you don't have to worry about him thinking you are "going over his head."

When I get nowhere with pseudo-decision makers I very quickly bypass them and reach out to others who might be involved before competitors jump on it. This is not only good for time management but also crucial to getting you to win deals.

Proposal Hell or Why I don't Write Proposals

If you are in a company where long proposals (more than 1 page long) are written or heck if any proposals are written shoot me an e-mail so I can convince your bosses why it's a fool's errand. I've seen companies where proposals are written by sales people because that's a metric that is used to measure sales performance! You can guess what comes next – that's right, the close ratio on those proposals is miniscule. Proposals don't sell. People do. When people ask me to send a proposal I say "Well if I send you a proposal that is 10 pages long, because you are a busy executive, you will look at the cover page for a second and then you will go to the last page and look at the dollar amount because that's what I would do and that's what most decision makers do. Why don't I come out there and present to your decision making committee and address issues that are really the crux of the matter and of crucial importance to our mutual success and collaboration?"

This is a bold rejection of the status quo and it works unless you are working with a government agency or some large company that demands a proposal because they want to renew a contract with an incumbent vendor but internal processes of "fairness" require that they get three bids. In essence you are completely wasting your time when you just jump right to a proposal without knowing who is going to review it, why do they need a proposal, who else is participating in the bid, is there a possibility nobody will get awarded the bid, etc. In my life, the longer the proposals I wrote and the higher the dollar amount in question in those proposals, I lost the deals. I lost the deals because I wasn't following the methodology that proposals don't sell and truly understanding that proposals are not even read! Proposals that do get read receive such a perfunctory treatment that it's a slap on the face of the hours of work you put into writing the proposal. You put in hours and hours of work and they spend 45 seconds skimming through it, if that. Unless you are working for Lockheed Martin and the government of Germany is asking for a bid on a $50 billion award for fighter jets you don't need to write a proposal to win a deal.

If the client protests and says "Your competitor submitted a proposal" I would reply with "John, I would be happy to come by and compare our solution to that of our competitors line item by line item so you can make a fully informed decision with complete confidence. From my experience, our unique set of services provides a value-add that none of our competitors can match. However, if writing a proposal is mandatory to earn your business, I would like to deliver the proposal in person and compare it with all the competitors who have turned in a proposal. What date/time works for you?"

Closing or Make Sure to Ask for the Sale

People who are not experienced in sales think closing skills is a unique set of skills in and of themselves. In the B2B sales context, everything that precedes the actual close determines the ease of closure. In other words, if you've followed methodology up until the point of closure then the deal will close with ease as long as you ask for the sale. Closing is not one isolated action that occurs at the end of the sales process. It's a continuous set of binary choices you offer to the client at each step of the sales process. That is to say, you get a "yes" or a "no" many times during the sales process towards the final "yes." For example, when you secure you a meeting you have closed the client on a meeting. When you ask for the client's buy-in to involve all the decision makers and he agrees, you have closed the client on a key step in the decision making process. All these mini-closures lead to the final closure of the deal.

At the final closure of the deal you are essentially confirming the following in a meeting or a call by summarizing to the client the set of steps that occurred up until now:

- Client has stated a problem or you have identified problems or solutions that they did not think of but were interested in – list those problems
- You have established the impact of doing nothing and/or doing something to solve the problems – list and quantify those benefits
- Re-cap the decision factors the decision makers and stakeholders found important and how your company is addressing those factors
- Discuss the proposed solution and how it will solve the problem(s)
- Re-cap agreed upon timelines
- Re-cap agreement on price

- Make closing statement: "In order to proceed we will need a signature on this contract. Will you be able to get this signed off on today?" (this closing statement and sign-off date will vary depending on terms and prior conversations on how the client makes a purchase but essentially you will be asking for the sale)

If at this last stage some decision maker throws a spanner in the deal remain calm and find out what objections they have and deal with those objections. If you've done your due diligence there shouldn't be any objections at this stage but once in a while you might encounter a late-stage twist. Just remain calm and address the client's concerns and then proceed again to ask for the sale.

Sometimes you have to deal with people in procurement at closure. If the buyer directs you to procurement you usually won't have too much trouble from them. They'll just need some standard paperwork to set you up (if it's a new client) and they might ask for certificates of insurance which you can get from your company.

Price is Rarely the Main Issue and How Not to Drop your Pants

I have run into senior sales people who do not know how to sell on value and therefore always fret about the price. They fret about the price before the deal, during the deal, and after the deal. They don't want to quote without discounting. Even after you show those sales people time and again that deals are closed at retail rates or higher they still don't get it. It's a serious mental block that is difficult to treat. If anyone should have a problem with the price it should be the client. Clients in turn have trained sales people to think that price is the main issue when it rarely is the main issue. It might be *one* of the issues but usually it is not the main issue. The majority of the companies in the market that are successful are selling on value – whether in B2C or B2B. Apple doesn't sell the cheapest phones (B2C) and GE does not sell the cheapest engines (B2B). It's not (only) about price. You as a sales person should be comfortable selling at high prices because unless you're selling a bare-bones generic product and working for a company that sells on price (which is not the norm) then you should learn how to conduct dialogue with the client on value. It's actually much easier than you think. Clients know the old adage "you get what you pay for" and so in today's buying environment they aren't looking for the best price but for the best value. What they are really looking for is peace of mind and a solution to the pain they are experiencing.

Clients might, as a buying strategy, ask for a discount. It's not uncommon for procurement people to ask for discounts because they are professional buyers and have gone to "negotiation school." Many sales people panic when the client asks for a discount. They do everything to appease the client. I've seen people at the level of general management who go to a meeting with a savvy buyer or a procurement rep who was just doing his due diligence by asking for a discount and the general manager or sales rep dropped the price by an arbitrarily large (and cringeworthy) 30% on the spot without any value exchange. I've even seen a deal where a senior rep buckled and discounted a deal from $200,000 to $110,000 because the client very nonchalantly asked for a discount. The client did not say "I want a $90,000 discount." He just asked for a discount! Not only is that worthy of a firing but it also tells me that the sales person did not know the first thing about value. Not only did the sales person take away a huge chunk of commissions from their own income in that one moment of incoherent thinking but also cost the company she was representing significant profits. Worst of all it communicated to the client that the service was not worth

$200,000. There were no competitors in the deal and the client's need was urgent and important. Had she not discounted or given the client a token 1% discount she would have still won the deal.

Here's how you never drop yours pants when you are asked for a discount. Firstly, understand that the client is just doing their job by seeking a token discount (most clients don't even ask for a discount any more). Secondly, remain calm! Thirdly, re-explain to them the value of the service and how the results they will achieve far outweigh the amount being charged for the deal. Then ask for the sale again. If they still balk and ask for a discount, ask them what they are expecting. At this point the client might throw a number like 5% or whatever. Don't buckle! Say something like this: "John, I am only authorized to discount this service by 2%. Can we shake hands to that?" Quite often the client will be happy because they feel they accomplished something in the negotiation and you'll get the deal. If the client does not budge then say "Please allow me to consult with my boss for a minute but before I do, if I am able to secure you a 5% discount, and I'm not saying I can, do we have a deal?"

In essence you are getting something for something. Do not give away something and get nothing in return! If you discount a service get something back in return and these can include:
- Extended commitment (2 years versus 1 years for example)
- Video testimonials (the client promoting your product or service)
- Immediate commitment (will you be able to sign today?)
- Reduction of elements of the service (your after-hours support will be reduced by 25% for example)
- Immediate payment (instead of net 30)

I can write a few chapters on the discounting problem and how it decimates entire industries by starting price wars just because some revenue officer in the C-suite had a (ridiculous) compensation plan that tied bonuses to movement of inventory. It not only kills the company but kills competitors who follow suit.

The Universe of Objections and How to Overcome Them

There is a finite list of objections prospects raise and you should be aware of every single one of them and your response to those should be smooth and practiced. If your objections cannot be overcome because it's just a dead end then always get referrals by asking "Well, John, thank you for your time and I appreciate that our services might not be a good fit for you. Can you think of colleagues who might benefit?"

I've already covered the pricing and discount objections and how to deal with them. Here are a few more common objections:

Client: Why don't you send me a brochure?
Respond: John, if I mail you a brochure, more than likely it will end up in the trash bin after a quick glance. Instead, can you tell me what's really important to you to achieve this year? (I actually used this and the client chuckled and opened up with an opportunity)

Client: I will keep your information on file
Respond: Thank you for that. John, I have never managed to graduate from someone's file to actually doing business with them. Can you tell me what's really important for you to accomplish this year?

Client: Call me later. I'm busy.
Respond: John, I totally understand. Does 3:30 pm today work? (or if he's not rushing to get you off the phone say: John, that's totally understandable. Could we schedule a brief meeting in-person this Thursday at 9:00 am? If that doesn't work I'm open

to alternate time slots that work for you).

Client: Call me six months from now.
Respond: I can definitely do that. If I may ask, is there some type of timeline or budgetary constraint that you foresee will free up six months from now that makes that a more appropriate time frame for a discussion?
Client: Yes / No.
Respond: I see. Well, just so we know if we should even be talking and I don't pester you six months from now and find out it's not a good fit, would you have a couple of minutes to go over some specifics? (At this stage, find out preliminary needs, value prop statement, and schedule meeting if appropriate).

Client: I don't see any value in your product or service.
Respond: John, thank you for the frank feedback. It helps us improve our service portfolio. Can you tell me what's really important to you to achieve this year and what would be a true value-add? (Here you will uncover that the client either does not understand your value-add in which case you'll have to explain it by quantifying it or your client has identified an area of need in which your company doesn't have anything valuable to contribute in which case you bring it to the attention of the managers in your company to see if said service can be added to the portfolio or if you can partner with someone to provide the service).

Client (in bid situations): You cannot see the decision maker. It wouldn't be fair to other competitors.
Respond: John, I appreciate that. But I've seen in such situations companies provide solutions that don't match the needs of the decision makers. I want to be fair to us and you by finding out what truly matters to your decision makers so I can propose a

solution that will get you the results you are seeking. If fairness is the issue, feel free to share the information that you share with me with our competitors.

Client: Your service is missing this crucial piece that we are looking for
Respond: John, thanks for sharing that. I'm sorry I must have missed that this was a critical need for the success of this project. If we incorporate this to our proposed solution, and adjust the pricing accordingly, would you be willing to work with us on this project?

Client: We already use ABC (competitor) company
Respond: And that's fine. We've worked with several clients who have also used our competitor's products. Our product has some key differences that have led to making our client's lives much easier through increased productivity. Some have totally switched over to us because it made such a difference and I'm confident it will give you some food for thought at the very least. Would you have some time next Monday for me to come out and discuss specifics (or offer a virtual meeting if you are a remote sales person).

You will hear dozens of other objections which more or less can be classified into broader categories which I covered above. Respond accordingly by understanding in which category the client's objections falls.

The Problem of Anchoring

Don't talk prices early on in the sales process unless it's in terms of ballparks as mentioned earlier in the book. I've seen sales people make the mistake of saying things like "Oh, we did a delivery just like this for a client for 400 people and it cost less than $30,000." This is a rookie mistake for several reasons.

Firstly, no two deals are similar. Secondly, that particular deal in question which the sales person compared to could have been seriously discounted. Thirdly, the client "anchors" any subsequent deal you have with him to that $30,000 figure. This is a problem of anchoring and you must do your best to avoid it. This also explains why I'm against "end-of-year" blow out sales discounts because it creates an inventory imbalance problem (sometimes called a bullwhip effect) and it trains the client to wait to make purchases from you at the end of the year and anchors that price to you and hampers the value creation process.

How to Get Paid Quickly or Show me the Scrilla

Many sales people get the sale and then forget about collecting on the sale. If you're in B2C this isn't a problem because customers pay with a credit card or some payment plan handled by financing. In B2B this is a serious problem. If not managed properly a company can start having cash flow problems and end up in a vicious borrowing cycle to make payroll and suchlike. You as a sales person have a fiduciary responsibility to ensure prompt and timely payment – especially if you are compensated on collections (versus sales). I've seen many sales people whose invoices linger on in the aging reports (receivables) and the company has to spend resources tracking down where the invoice is and whether the client received it and make calls to get paid, etc. Pre-emptively crush those time-wasting soul-draining money-chasing dilemmas.

You set the tone at the time of closing the deal by asking for payment on a credit card or via ACH. If neither of those options work then get paid by check within 10 to 30 days (unless it's a multi-phased ongoing billing type of deal in which case get paid weekly through weekly invoicing). By asking for payment on a credit card (or p-card as clients in B2B will often call it) you are getting paid at the outset even before services are delivered. This is an ideal scenario. The only drawback is that your company has to pay a 2% to 3.5% fee or thereabouts for credit card processing. That stings but it's much more costly for a company to chase down payment for outstanding invoices. My favorite method is ACH because you set up your vendor account with your client's accounts payable department such that they electronically transfer funds from their account to your company's bank account and there is no fee for it. Administrative costs are minimal and you just have to agree to terms (payment is due at the time of signing of contract, or within 10 days, or 30 days at the latest). Some companies, especially large ones, may strong arm you into accepting net 45 terms (or I've even seen net 75). If you accept those terms (and I have) I make sure those are a tiny minority of my client portfolio and that they are good customers to work with. You don't want to get 45 days out and deal with an ornery client. Also, always ask for shorter terms even if they offer net 30 or net 45. If you don't ask, your probability of getting it is 0%. If you ask, the probability of getting a concession is way above 0%.

If you cannot get the client to accept either the credit card or ACH method you will be forced to send an invoice out and get paid by check. Here's what you do to ensure you get paid on time. E-mail the invoice (don't snail mail it). If there is a purchase order number ensure that the number shows on the invoice. If you have a vendor number make sure that shows on the invoice. If you have agreed to payment terms of net 15 then don't write net 15. Write out the actual payment due date. Next, don't call the client but call the accounts payable department and say "Hi Joanna, I'm calling with XYZ Company and we wanted to ensure our current invoices are in your system. Could you please confirm that invoice # 6123 for the amount of $45,000 is in your system and set for payment on February 15th? The PO number is 45699-12." Guess what? The accounts payable people are usually very easy to work with and will give you all the information you need. You want to call as soon as the invoice is sent. Don't wait until it is already due because you might find out that it's not even in the system and you have to wait another few weeks to get paid. I have seen countless times when companies received payment late because this pre-emptive step of checking that the invoice is actually in the system was not followed.

Understand that several steps have to occur in the client's work flow for your invoice to get paid and you want to make sure you push it through to the step of the invoice actually being in the system. Sometimes even after it is in the system a manager has to approve the invoice and AP may be waiting on that sign-off. You might have to gently ping a manager to get his sign off if he has not done it and usually they will quickly get it done for you. Sometimes CFO's will manage cash flow by paying vendors late in what is a malevolent business practice that can crush small businesses. If that happens to you have your senior executives have a heart to heart discussion with such a client and explain that you love working with them but not getting paid on time makes it difficult to do business. Usually a friendly heart to heart chat will get your company on the "exception list" and you'll get paid on time.

Dis-Invite Legal from the Party

Clients sometimes invoke their legal departments to review contracts. This is understandable if it's a sophisticated service with many nuances. If your product or service is simple then work with the client to bypass legal and get a simple agreement form signed or just get something in writing in an e-mail. I recommend you do this with repeat trustworthy clients so that you can bypass legal. The problem with legal is that it usually prolongs the sales process. Your clients, just like you, often don't want legal involved because they want to get their problems solved as quickly as possible. Allow innovative options for example: "John, I understand you can't sign any contract without having it go through legal. I tell you what – since the services are needed starting Monday I'll accept your payment as a substitute for a signed contract with the understanding that the services as outlined in our meetings and e-mails is what's being sold and I can summarize that in an e-mail so we're all on the same page." You will find that clients who don't like legal dragged in on a deal are willing to just pay for the services and you should accept that as a contract for repeat clients.

If you're selling an ERP that costs millions of dollars you'll have legal join the dance and you do want that for the protection of both parties. Use your judgment. I will tell you that I closed tons of deals without any cumbersome contracts and legalese and delivered millions of dollars of services without having legal involved. By paying with a credit card the client established good will and it never blew back on my face.

Recency, Frequency, and Dollar Amounts

As you progress in your career you will have a portfolio of clients and you will notice that most of the sales come from a small percentage of your client portfolio. Known as the 80/20 rule or the Pareto principle this distribution shows up in many things in life.

The three most important factors that influence the likelihood of future sales from a given client are recency, frequency, and size of prior deals. By recency I mean that recent clients will also likely buy more from you than an old client of yours who hasn't purchased in more than a year. Clients who have purchased with greater frequency are also likelier to purchase from you in the future. Clients who have invested significant money with you are also likely to continue purchasing more. There are many other variables to consider such as service quality, one-offs, macroeconomic factors, etc. But in general, recency, frequency, and high dollar amount clients are indicators of the likelihood of future sales from any given client. Allocate sufficient time to nurture those clients. When sales people are in doldrums and not sure who to call I ask them to look at recency, frequency, and dollar amounts to know whose door to knock on again.

It intuitively makes sense to follow up and nurture those relationships that keep producing. Often, additional opportunities will pop up in follow up conversations with clients with whom you just wrapped up a project or delivery. While delivering solutions you will often uncover additional problems or opportunities just in the course of being engaged with the client. Take advantage of nurturing and feeding those accounts.

Clients Like Talking About Themselves

This is an elaboration of my rule to let the client talk 80% or more of the time. The top sales guys talk the least and *they talk to the client about the client* and guide the client to talk about themselves instead of taking easy refuge in talking about their products and services. Think about it. The universe of discussion points around the client's projects, their roles, their company, their growth, their challenges, etc. is far greater in sheer volume and content than any one company's products or services ever could be. The former is also far more interesting to clients (and to elite sales people). Let that balance show in the conversation. Speak less. Less is more. Internalize that for success.

Again and again I keep seeing mediocre salespeople take refuge and comfort in talking on and on and on about their products and services. Telling isn't selling and less is more. Don't get me wrong. I'm not saying don't talk about your product and services at all. You should and you must. But do it after the client has described in detail what they care about. Also, when you do talk about your products and services be passionate and persuasive and make sure the client s*ees* and understands how it matches up with their problems and how it will make their lives better and how it will make them look good in their organization. It's ultimately about them, not about you or your products.

<u>*If You Sense it Say it (Tactfully)*</u>

If you sense something is left unsaid help your case by probing the matter gently with the client. Re-direct conversations back to the client as much as possible so that the client speaks the majority of the time. Often I see clients ask sales people questions that require an obvious re-direction but mediocre sales people are unable to re-direct. Here's an example:

Client: Does your company help with change management?
Mediocre sales person: Definitely. We are experts in change management and use all kinds of frameworks. Matter of fact, we just completed a change management project for a client that was struggling with an ERP adoption challenge and…(on and on and on)

Now look at how an elite sales person would re-direct:

Client: Does your company help with change management?
Elite sales person: Yes. May I ask what made you mention change management?

Both sales people sense that there might be a change management project in the offing but one of them starts taking refuge in "telling is selling" and droning on and on about how they are the best in change management while the other rapidly shifts attention back to the client.

As a sales person you must become really good at re-directing attention back to the client and question things that may be left hanging unanswered. Frequently I ask the most obvious questions to sales people about opportunities and they haven't the slightest clue because they didn't bother probing the client or questioning assumptions. Here are a few things clients might say which should trigger your "if you sense it say it" alert system:

Client: I can't get anything approved here
You: How do you mean?

Client: My boss will not approve this
You: Sounds like you've had prior experience with that. How do you propose we proceed?

Client: This software won't work
You: What makes you say that?

Client: I want results yesterday!
You: Given the high visibility of this project, clearly getting results immediately is important to you. Realistically speaking how soon can we start on this project and what is the latest we can get you the deliverables and still make this project a success?

Client: I need three more team members this quarter.
You: Otherwise…?

Client: Your price is too high
You: Thank you for your frank feedback. May I ask what you are comparing our price to?

Client: They will never let this deal through
You: Who do you mean and why do you think they would block the deal?

Communication is the Lubricant Redux

Communication skills are a recurring theme in this book and for good reason. It's one of the top three take away points from this book. Less is more. Telling isn't selling. Precision counts. Concision counts. Do not be afraid of pregnant pauses and understand the power of silence. Most sales people are terrified when a conversation with a client leads to silence and they start yammering to fill in the space. Silence is a powerful and necessary component of dialogue. It allows the client to marinate on what is being said. It allows them to reflect. It allows you to reflect on the gravity of their problem. I often say "Hmm" or "Remarkable" and nod my head and stay silent in client meetings. Clients appreciate that. To them it's a refreshing change. To them it's somebody who is finally listening to them. Don't be afraid of silence. Use it.

What do I mean by "precision counts"? It means don't be vague but rather be specific. Here's a difference between a mediocre sales man and a precise sales man:

Mediocre sales man: John, I can't even begin to tell you, you know, this is a great instrument. It's the sharpest we got. It'll give you the most bang for your buck, see. It's a swell instrument John. Better than all of our competitors.

Precise sales man: John, our T-500 provides 30% sharper resolution than the M70 you are currently using and is 15% sharper than the X50 – our closest competitor in the market. It will reduce your re-work by 50% and increase throughput by 70% thus saving you $650,000 this fiscal year which is $200,000 higher than your desired target.

What do I mean by "concision counts"? It means that don't say things in a long-winded way. Look at the difference:

Mediocre sales man: Well, you know, if you get it to me by today I'll talk to our operations and see Susan is off the next two days. Yeah, she's having a grandson over the weekend. I know, right?! When she gets back I'll have a chat with her and depending on how things are I'll get it back to you by Friday, at the latest. Man, I'm going to Lake Wobegon on Friday too. Have you been out there yonder?

Concise sales man: John, do you think you can get those figures to me by today? Great. In that case, you should have the deliverables by Friday the 16th. Will that work?...Excellent. Thanks for working with us.

Communication precision, concision, poise, and smoothness are so important to becoming an elite sales person. I'm not saying don't ever get into friendly banter but you want to keep that to a minimum. Clients are extremely busy and you should be respectful of their time and your own time. Concision, precision, and silence are powerful tools of communication.

3 THE COLLEAGUE

The colleagues are the third and final leg of the tripod of sales success. By colleagues I mean people who are in your professional life and affect your sales (but are not the first two tripods of "The Self" and "The Client"). This includes your work colleagues, bosses, suppliers, partners, mentors, etc. The important thing to note here is that you must use your network of colleagues to further your sales and not let them become an impediment.

Good Bosses and Bosses from Hell

Everyone seems to encounter horrible bosses in their lives but just like anything in life there are good ones and bad ones. Regardless of whether you get a good boss or a horrible one you must know that after managing "The Self" you must manage everyone around you and that includes managing upwards when it comes to bosses and managing downwards when it comes to whomever reports to you and managing sideways with everyone else.

Good bosses are usually kind and give you freedom to sell. The best bosses are intelligent and have a good awareness of the market. Your immediate boss will likely be a sales manager who might report to a division head or a VP or a general manager. Good sales managers only intervene when you are behind and they are excellent resources and good sounding boards. They are like good coaches who show you the possibilities and help instill within you a sense of discipline and hold you accountable when you do not meet quota. Dealing with your sales manager on a day to day basis should be uneventful. They may parcel out inbound leads, monitor your pipeline, and hold review meetings on current deals. Sales managers might join you for meetings and conference calls. Inform the sales manager about what you need to help you succeed especially if you are stuck. The top sales guys usually call the shots on the sales floor and sales managers follow their lead especially on conference calls or meetings. That power dynamic is important. Once I became seasoned in sales I did not "report" to any sales manager even if I had a reporting relationship. I was given carte blanche to bring home the bison and sales managers did everything they could to support me. That's the position you want to be in where your boss becomes your collaborator and you both work in concert to increase revenue. Help them help you. Excite them to the possibilities. It's a symbiotic relationship that can and should flourish.

Your boss' boss may or may not interact much with the sales people directly. They might have Profit & Loss (P & L) responsibility and are more concerned with running the business. Have a good relationship with the big bosses all the way up to the owners or C-suite. This is important because if you have a horrible boss somewhere in the middle of the chain of bosses then you know people who know people who know to take care of the problem. More importantly, you need to know the entire chain of bosses because one day you will, if you are ambitious enough, take their spot when they retire or leave and you will take the company forward. If you get market signals about your products or services that are negative, then don't fume or complain. Use it as an opportunity to present to top management about how this presents a pivot point to launch new services or modify existing services to satisfy the clients. If you present it in a mature and intelligent way your bosses will notice and appreciate you. Even if you're not in the empire building business then your path to selling will remain smooth and your sales manager will not throw obstacles at you. Managing upwards will make you indispensable to your company. Managing upwards takes shrewdness and a keen awareness of people's strengths and weaknesses. Never back bite your superiors or criticize them in front of anyone. You can criticize things behind doors in confidence but not out in the open. When you do criticize make it very constructive and always ensure that you are talking about how to move the company forward. The ones who don't move up the chain are those who constantly criticize other people. Managing upwards becomes smoother when you project confidence, knowledge, and have a positive can-do attitude.

You might think I've had smooth sailing with bosses all my life. Au contraire! At one point in my career I had a certifiable crackpot of a horrible boss. The fellow was funny and charming but had psychotic episodes and megalomania (and later I found out he was on medication for his psychological problems). Full of arrogance and cockiness, this horrible boss was a royal pain in everyone's butt including mine but he had accumulated power in the company. He made death threats, was loud and boisterous, waddled around proclaiming "god is me and I am god", regularly bashed a file cabinet with his golf club while sales people were on the phone trying to earn a living, "danced" like a fat version of Elvis at company parties, terrorized junior sales reps, stalked the personal phone records of female employees, spent time procuring "services" at the local exotic club during lunch, and bribed premiere client contacts with cash (and boasted about it). All the while upper management just could not see through him because headquarters was in a different city and he played nice in front of top brass. Finally, one day I had had enough when he cut off my access to CRM and told me all my accounts would be transferred to other sales reps and I'd have to start from scratch on Monday. Along with other sales people I orchestrated his ouster from the company. He left threatening to take all the clients with him to a competitor. A law enforcement official had to be brought in to guard the company for three days in case that crackpot returned to stir up trouble. After he joined the competitor they figured him out within a few months and dropped him like a hot potato. He joined a series of competitors lasting only a few months at each company. Horrible bosses like these are so delusional that they post their strengths on LinkedIn as "Servant Leader" and "Humbleness."

At another time I worked at a franchise where the corporate CEO traveled in for a visit. He was courteous but wasn't very forward thinking or innovative. During his tenure competitors and start-ups in the same space with forward thinking ideas and impeccable execution ate his lunch. The CEO was so disconnected from the company that during the annual conference in Vegas to honor top sales people in the global network he stumbled and forgot one of the mission or vision statements a la Rick Perry's "oops" moment. Nevertheless, I remember I had e-mailed him a "thank you" note for personally visiting the franchise and I provided some recommendations on market opportunities and strategies. The guy who was second in command to the CEO did not like that and complained to the franchise manager about it and I got an earful. Compare and contrast this to companies where ideas from employees are actively solicited and flourish into billion dollar businesses (like Google as just one example of many). The second-in-command guy did his own flying around to franchises. His steely blue eyes were tired and his posture resigned. He spent days doing S.W.O.T. analyses with franchise owners but didn't have the slightest of clues of how to marry S.W.O.T. to corporate level strategies of retrenchment, turn-arounds, etc. He was making a cool $700,000 salary or thereabouts and he couldn't be bothered except to go through the motions. He didn't last in the company and these days does similar work for a tutoring franchise.

If you have horrible bosses you can throw up your hands and say "I quit" and you might well be justified. Or you tell yourself that as long as you are a star performer you should not let their incompetence bother you. This choice of which battles you pick with colleagues will be a key determinant of your success.

Some sales people and managers are cheerleading company-men and the quintessential "yes-men" who proclaim that the sky is green if the higher-ups say the sky is green. It is better to be silent than to say yes to something with which you disagree. Ideally, you want to be working at companies that truly make their mark in the economy and who value clever divergent thinkers and impressive executioners. Companies with filled with "yes-men" fall into possibly fatal group think. Companies with divergent thinkers (like Google) are innovation hubs and are constantly coming up with new products that delight customers.

I have had my share of good bosses. At one company I worked I heard the new CEO (and co-owner) was a man from Louisiana whose net worth was well north of $20 million and his partner reportedly had a net worth in excess of $100 million. But he was one of the humblest men I had ever met. He was a classic hard worker who overcame adversities and turned his life around. He even embarrassed me once by saying "I might be working for you one day" even though I was decades junior to him. I never encountered a shred of arrogance in him and he was always respectful of ideas you shared.

In addition to working collaboratively with your sales manager you must know his strengths and weaknesses. Is he unjust in his division of leads and do you think he is displaying nepotism? Then challenge him to distribute leads equally for an entire month and tell him to measure the close ratio. This happened to me once and I was able to show the sales manager by the end of two months that I had the highest close ratio of all sales people which led to a more equitable distribution of leads.

Just remember one thing when you deal with colleagues – life is not fair. But you can win despite the unfairness. I remember when I was a fresh salesperson on a floor of twenty two sales people there were two women who could barely stitch together a sentence let alone communicate with clients coherently. One of those ladies was a cousin of the sales manager. Yet these ladies were pulling in impressive sales. There was a lot of back-dooring going on and the sales manager was helping out the cousin because "blood is thicker than water." Rumors were flying but nobody could really do anything about it. Soon the sales manager returned to becoming a salesman and the ladies no longer had the Cadillac treatment. Their sales started suffering immediately and they eventually could not make it. When you encounter open or clandestine nepotism like this remember one thing – one or two people being favored is not an excuse for you not performing well because sales is not a zero-sum game. In other words, just because she sold $80,000 this month I'm going to sell $20,000 because the whole pie is $100,000. It is not like that at all. The size of the pie is itself malleable and it is up to you to succeed or fail. Also, keep in mind that sales managers generally reward and reinforce good selling behavior and outcomes because they are compensated based on total team sales. So if they notice you are selling well they will help you because it is ultimately in their interest.

Bear in mind that nothing is set in stone. I was at a company once where the commissions were 15%. However, I had worked a deal with a channel partner that led to revenue for the partner in excess of $1 million and all the work and service delivery was being done by the partner. As part of the revenue sharing agreement I was able to post more than $100,000 in sales from this deal. But because I was never a yes-man I said to myself "Hmm…our company is not lifting a finger to deliver the services tied to the sales I just posted so why am I seeing only 15% of commission?" I then went home and strategized and came up with the right things to say to my boss and boss's boss so that the owner accepted a commission of 20% on that deal (I had asked for 25% instead of 15%). This was an exception no sales person was ever given before and I suspect it was because they never asked nor did they carefully plan out how to make it a win-win for themselves and the company.

Another time, a sales rep had departed and a key account was there for the taking (or inheriting an account as it was called). Based on performance, only two sales reps could inherit this account – either me or another guy who went on later to become top sales guy globally at a company. The person who would make the decision as to who would inherit the account was the aforementioned "horrible" boss with psychotic proclivities. My colleague, the top rep, went to the sales manager (aka horrible boss) and made his case. Then he approached me and over lunch consoled me in preparation for him taking over the account. I had yet to make my approach to the sales manager. I preferred going second because what he would hear last would be more front-of-mind and because I knew exactly what I had to say. Firstly, I knew the sales manager had a massive ego and was looking for upward mobility to the General Manager position (which he never was able to secure because of his ouster). Secondly, I knew how important that meeting with the sales manager was to me personally because that 10 minute meeting could mean an extra $30,000 in income (commissions) the following month. Thirdly, I knew that I would have to cater to his emotional needs in order to inherit the account. At this point in my career I was just moving up the ranks. I went in there and told him how the international conference was coming up and everyone was looking forward to meeting him and that the big bosses were looking at consolidating his position in the company. I asked him "Wouldn't it be great if you had two President's Club Members representing our territory at the international conference instead of just one?" I told him that if I inherited the account having him shine at the international conference and look good in front of the big bosses would be a foregone conclusion. I spent the entire meeting helping him visualize how great he could be. This is because I followed the sales methodology of knowing who the decision maker is and what his criteria for decision making was! If it was a normal sales manager I would have made a different case about account growth, company growth, profitability, my network of contacts in other accounts that knew the contacts in this account that was to be inherited, etc. But I left all of that out in my meeting and sure enough I was awarded the account. The top sales rep who had pre-maturely consoled me was dumb founded and I simply smiled and went back to work.

Operations

In many companies there is a healthy (and necessary) tension between sales and operations. Sales people want revenue no matter what. Operations wants to keep costs down no matter what. Operations also has to do a lot of juggling, shuffling, forecasting, and resource management that most sales people do not understand. The power dynamic in companies usually favors sales people because they are the "father who brings home the bread and thus must be honored and cherished." Sales is the glamour job and operations is the engine room. If you're good in sales you'll generally receive good treatment and high upward mobility.

When you deal with operations be courteous and friendly. Show them respect unless they openly disrespect you. Help them help you by making it easy for them to serve you. If operations requires certain pieces of information from you as a standard matter of protocol then don't whine about it. Just give them the information they need so they can respond to you as quickly as possible. If operations is in the same building walk over to them and foster a nice working relationship with them. Don't write passive aggressive e-mails and sarcastic text messages to them. If you show them you appreciate them they will be eager to help you. If you show them how a potential deal you're working on will make a difference they will be eager to help you. If you think the current process is a piece of ancient junk written and formulated in a bygone era then propose a working meeting where both sales and operations works together to come up with a new work flow. Be part of the solution if you are pointing out a problem.

Other Salespeople

Your fellow sales people have a strong impact in the way you think about sales and your company. Associate yourself with sales people who are better than you so you can learn best practices from them. Don't waste time with the mediocre reps who are talking about meaningless things that do not help you further your career. Do not get into arguments with sales people. I have seen the weirdest things happen between sales people – from intra-office romance to nitwits falling for Nigerian prince scams to money laundering to cocaine usage to useless chit chat and negative discourse. I even witnessed two sales guys who almost came to blows in a corporate cafeteria over whether the justice system is fair to minorities. Extricate yourself from all this "noise" and be laser focused on your success and learn from the best.

Partner Relationships

Not every company has channel partners but if you do make it a point to go to lunch with them. Exchange valuable information about what's happening in accounts and tag team on accounts if that helps your sales. This is unorthodox but it can work as long as your company has no conflicts. I have been able to secure deals for channel partners and in return get a revenue share.

Suppliers

You will normally not be dealing with suppliers as a sales person but if you ever encounter them or talk to them, foster a good relationship with them and find out what they are seeing in the market. Some suppliers have close relationships with sales people because they might be delivering an integral part of a broader solution. In those cases you should know who these suppliers are and what they do and what's important to them and how you can help each other succeed.

Assistants

Assistants can be a God-send. First rule with assistants is don't get involved in a non-professional relationship with your assistant and do not harass her. Not just because that is against ethical norms and can possibly get your company in trouble legally but also because your assistant is not there for your entertainment. She is there to help you further your sales by taking on things from your priority quadrant that you should not be handling. She is there to screen calls from low level customers who might take time from you in dealing with an issue that she can take care of for you. Remember the rule of delegation – do only that which only you can do, delegate the rest. She is there to remove all kinds of administrative burdens that slow down the sales machine that you are. Be nice and friendly with your assistants and have a good sense of humor. Don't beat them up for small mistakes. Coach and train them to be the best they can be. Encourage their ambitions if they want to be something else or move up in their career. But remember one thing – don't get so friendly with them that they forget you are the boss. Your authority should be unquestioned and you must be respected.

This concludes the tripod of sales success.

Elite Sales People versus Mediocre Sales People

I've covered in detail the behavioral differences between elite sales people and mediocre sales people and I'll summarize the main differentiators here again:

- Elite sales people hunt lions and big prey. Mediocre sales people hunt squirrels and gerbils.
- Elite sales people are superb multi-layered listeners and can read between the lines. Mediocre sales people are listening to what's going on in their heads about what they want to say next to the client.
- Elite sales people connect the dots and look for patterns for more sales. Mediocre sales people are happy if they can just make quota and they worry about how they can pay bills.
- Elite sales people use their network of colleagues. Mediocre sales people think the system is against them.
- Elite sales people work constantly at harnessing "The Self" while mediocre sales people are negative whiners and look for outward blame.
- Elite sales people tightly adhere to methodology like snipers. Mediocre sales people often stray from proper methodology and shoot from the hip.
- Elite sales people are confident and polished. Mediocre sales people project lack of confidence and confusion about their products and services.
- Elite sales people call things out tactfully when clients say things that don't add up. Mediocre sales people don't go beyond surface level questioning of clients.
- Elite sales people consider sales as a prosperous career and stepping stone to financial freedom and executive

leadership. Mediocre sales people consider sales as just a job.
- Elite sales people are ferociously protective of their time. Mediocre sales people are often found loitering around water coolers.
- Elite sales people prioritize. Mediocre sales people are haphazard and think and act as if different activities are of equal priority.
- Elite sales people see clients as equals. Mediocre sales people see clients as superior.
- Elite sales people have excellent instincts for fishing out the truth and seriousness of a deal. Mediocre sales people clutch on to straw deals and don't have a keen sense of when a deal is valid.
- Elite sales people are friendly but keep clients at a professional arm's length. Mediocre sales people attempt to befriend clients and share personal details to their detriment.
- Elite sales people have good crisis resolution skills. Mediocre sales people are at a loss when dealing with crises.
- Elite sales people are ultimate enablers and facilitators of two-way dialogue. Mediocre sales people are stuck in a worm hole of one-way "telling is selling" fantasy.
- Elite sales people are global thinkers and know how to cross pollinate and upsell and cross sell. Mediocre sales people are localized thinkers and often fail to connect the dots and cross-sell.
- Elite sales people guide their clients on how to buy from them. Mediocre sales people seek guidance from clients and not very savvy on the intricacies of the buying process.
- Elite sales people bring novel ideas to the client and to their own companies thus adding tremendous value.

Mediocre sales people are stuck to a "catalog of our products and services" viewpoint.
- Elite sales people are always on the hunt to lock down clients in long term relationships through Master Services Agreements or other contracts and they protect their turf by engaging as many client contacts as possible. They make switching costs very high for the client. Mediocre sales people are more transactional thinkers and are happy with a sale here and a sale there.
- Elite sales people are full of grit and persevere in the face of adversity. Mediocre sales people give up too quickly when faced with resistance.

A Word on Business Development and Strategy for Sales

This section is geared towards managers and executives who interact with sales people and are in charge of the direction of a company. Strategizing is a job left for company strategists and C-level executives who need to pave the path forward for sales people to attack like the selling machines that they can be. Just as sales people are duty-bound to sell to the best of their ability, executives are duty-bound to keep their pulse on the market, innovate constantly, and be open to feedback from the front lines. Managers who manage out of ivory towers wallow in mediocrity throughout their careers and keep shifting laterally until they retire with a whimper. How do you avoid that?

Treat People with Respect and Dignity

Treat all employees, including sales people, with respect and dignity. When it comes to sales people you should know what balance of structure and discipline versus freedom they need to excel. Star sales people generally are self-motivated and highly goal-oriented and require minimal direction. The motto with them is "get out of the way." If you burden them with administrative work or put too many restrictions you will lose them to attrition.

Dr. Dan Ariely, a behavioral economist and psychologist in his book entitled "*Payoff: The Hidden Logic That Shapes our Motivations*", discusses the fascinating subject of motivations. A few of the key takeaways for managers include:
1. Make the nature of the work rewarding so the employees find joy and meaning in it and take a sense of ownership.
2. Don't stifle employees with too many rules. Instead trust them to be productive. Giving employees some degree of autonomy may seem counter-intuitive but it leads to more productivity.
3. Keep things challenging. If the work gets boring or

monotonous or too easy then employees lose steam and don't feel like they are living up to their potential.

4. Notes and expressions of appreciation can surprisingly be more effective than cash bonuses especially if the cash bonuses are tied to short-term goals. This goes back to treating people with respect and dignity and caring for their long-term well-being.

Don't short change your sales reps. I recall an egregious example of a sales rep at a Fortune 500 company who blew his quota in January with a monster sale. His commission on that deal alone was supposed to be in excess of $900,000. The management short changed him by paying him $125,000 instead because "that's too much commission to pay on one deal and it's only the beginning of the year." The sales person actually accepted the injustice and decided to buy a show horse with his earnings. You can tell that he was not an elite sales person and had gotten lucky with that one deal and was discounting the value he brought to his company. But the company lost the sales person soon and till today it has a bad reputation for having super-aggressive and arrogant sales people who are immersed in a macho culture. For a company's long-term success and growth the sure formula is to treat people with respect and dignity and help them find meaning in the work.

Mavens, Connectors, and Great Salespeople

Most executives don't realize that the difference between total market penetration and mediocre results is miniscule. Like the butterfly effect, only incremental improvements upstream make a massive impact on results downstream. In Dr. Wayne Winston's chapter entitled "The Mathematics Behind the Tipping Point"[1] there is conclusive evidence of this effect. He demonstrates quantitatively that connectors (people who know a lot of people), mavens (persuasive people who are knowledgeable about your product), and great sales people (which is what this book is about) are the three difference makers in a product or service's success. Even a modest increase in the length of time your product is spoken about and a slight increase in the persuasiveness of your sales people and a slight decrease in the resistance to your product cumulatively have a huge impact downstream in greatly increasing the sales of your product or service. Executives must think very hard about how to pull those levers and one of the obvious ones is training sales people to think and behave like elite sales people.

The One Year Look Back or Analyze This

Sales Managers should run reports or have reports run for them that give them a view on which customers purchased a year back in any given month. If for example you are in the month of March 2017 look back at sales made in March 2016 because often sales purchases are cyclical. It's important for sales people to follow up with clients who made purchases exactly a year back. This is in addition to ongoing priority "A" sales activities.

Sales and marketing data are extremely valuable. If you don't have a data analyst on staff then I suggest you learn how to analyze sales data because it will give you valuable insight into growth and early signals into stale product lines. In addition, analysis of sales data will give you a plethora of actionable insight to improve sales. Managers should be able to answer questions like the following fairly quickly:

1. What were my division's sales each of the last 60 months?

---

[1] Marketing Analytics, Wayne L. Winston, p. 644

2. Are there top revenue generating companies from two years ago or longer that are no longer a top account? Why not?
3. How have my division's sales trended the past 3 years?
4. Who are the top sales people and how have their sales trended?
5. Who are the sales people whose sales have trended downwards or below average and why?
6. What are my sales by geography and territory?
7. What are the gross profit margins of each of my product / service lines? How have they trended and why?
8. How have sales trended with my top revenue generating clients and why?
9. How are my forecasts compared to actual sales? Can I use a better forecasting method?
10. What are my competitors' sales in the same time periods?
11. Which clients take longer than 30 days to pay and can I get them to agree to new terms?
12. What time of the day and what day of the week are purchases made? (B2C)
13. What type of payment method is used? (percentages across various modes of payment)
14. What complementary product or service lines can I add without costly retrofitting?

Vision and Mission

Jim Collins' book "Built to Last" has startling examples of the importance of vision and mission. Everyone in the company should know these statements and how to go about executing them. The vision and mission are the soul of the company. There are far too many non-specific vision and mission statements I see in companies and executives often can't even articulate them. Take the time to truly work out your dual statements and live by them. Most companies treat this as an afterthought.

What is my Promise?

Clients buy based on what you promise about your product or service and not based on the product and service itself. Your sales people should thus know exactly what you are promising your clients and why they should bother to talk to them instead of a competitor.

Distribution Channels and an Ecosystem of Relationships

Distribution channels can make or break your company. Can you leverage a partner's distribution channel if yours is not mature enough? Have you considered every last distribution channel available to you? Are you using a direct sales force when e-commerce is more appropriate? Are you using resellers and affiliates and if so are you managing channel conflicts properly? Is there another region of the country or world where there is an untapped demand for your products and services? Executives must constantly be thinking of the bird's eye view and take a systemic approach.

Pivoting on your Products and Services

Take a good hard look at your suite of products and services. Analyze inside-out the profitability of each line and their time series trends. Look at your competitors' products and services and perform a cross-sectional analysis. If your product or service is non-differentiated and is not helping your customer reduce their costs or increase their margins better, faster, quicker, cheaper, or more reliably than your competitors then your sales people will have a tough time getting sales and you cannot blame them for it. Are sales of your products and services tied closely to unpredictable factors like commodity prices? Are you diversifying your products and services to mitigate such risks?

Are there new products and services you could launch cheaply on top of the existing infrastructure in response to client signals? Then don't be afraid to add those to your portfolio. If your sales have been going down year after year that's a major warning signal to pivot to what your clients really want. The best products and services are reverse engineered from client needs instead of the old "build and they will come" approach which results in rigid results that frustrate customers. This is especially true for software.

Lead and Disrupt

The majority of companies in the market are content to play catch up and follow the lead of the leader in product design, pricing, etc. The best defense is a good offense and bold leaders who take risks are those who manage to catapult their companies to the stratosphere (and sometimes they fail but it's worth taking the risk). If you are in a non-traditional line of business then disruption, change, and innovation are your bread and butter. Leading change can seem risky but being an also-ran or an imitator is riskier still.

Final Thoughts

I encourage you to re-read this book as you progress through your sales career as certain things will resonate more as you experience them first-hand. Sales is a rewarding career and constantly in high demand. The difference between being an average sales person and an elite sales person is a mind set and a set of behaviors that anyone can learn. I hope you are able to adopt the principles I shared in this book to take your career to the next level.

ABOUT THE AUTHOR

Archie T. Goldbacker is a businessman, sales coach, and management consultant. He holds an MBA from the University of Houston.

Contact: agoldbacker@gmail.com

www.ingramcontent.com/pod-product-compliance
Lightning Source LLC
Chambersburg PA
CBHW061440180526
45170CB00004B/1499